The Power of Life

AGAMBEN AND THE COMING POLITICS
(To Imagine a Form of Life, II)

David Kishik

Stanford University Press · Stanford, California

Stanford University Press
Stanford, California

Library of Congress Cataloging-in-Publication Data

Kishik, David, author.
  The power of life : Agamben and the coming politics (To imagine a form of life, II) /
David Kishik.
      pages cm
  Includes bibliographical references and index.
  ISBN 978-0-8047-7229-7 (cloth : alk. paper) — ISBN 978-0-8047-7230-3 (pbk. : alk.
paper)
    1. Agamben, Giorgio, 1942– 2. Political science—Philosophy. 3. Philosophy, Modern.
I. Title.
  B3611. A44K57 2012
  195—dc22
                                    2011013706

Typeset by Bruce Lundquist in 9/15 Palatino with Walbaum display

The Power of Life

Contents

Acknowledgments

The philosophy of life is a strange field to navigate, but it becomes even more disorienting when your guide is a living philosopher. I would like to thank Giorgio Agamben for making this endeavor as captivating as it was liberating.

My heartfelt gratitude goes to those who, in the roles of readers and editors, made this a much better book: Mathew Abbott, Roy Ben Shai, Adam Brown, Emily-Jane Cohen, Ricky Crano, Nathan Everson, T. Fleischmann, Pavel Godfrey, Cynthia Lindlof, Yoni Molad, Idris Robinson, and last (though in all other respects first), Netta Yerushalmy.

I was not entirely surprised to discover that Wittgenstein and Agamben, my "philosophical parents" to whom I have dedicated my first two books, happened to be born on the same day as my actual mother and father. This book is dedicated to my parents, who gave me what philosophy cannot.

. . .

Essays based on parts of this book appeared in *Allesdurchdringung: Texte, Essays, Gespräche über den Tanz*, ed. Andreas Hiepko (Berlin: Merve Verlag, 2008); *New Nietzsche Studies* 8 (2010); and *Telos* 150 (2010). Presentations based on parts of this book were delivered at conferences at Binghamton University, New York University, and University of Massachusetts Boston.

Abbreviations of Agamben's Major Works

CC   *The Coming Community*. Translated by Michael Hardt. Minneapolis: University of Minnesota Press, 1993.

EP   *The End of the Poem: Studies in Poetics*. Translated by Daniel Heller-Roazen. Stanford: Stanford University Press, 1999.

HS   *Homo Sacer: Sovereign Power and Bare Life* (*Homo Sacer*, I). Translated by Daniel Heller-Roazen. Stanford: Stanford University Press, 1998.

IH   *Infancy and History: The Destruction of Experience*. Translated by Liz Heron. London: Verso, 2007.

IP   *Idea of Prose*. Translated by Michael Sullivan and Sam Whitsitt. Albany: State University of New York Press, 1995.

KG   *The Kingdom and the Glory: For a Theological Genealogy of Economy and Government* (*Homo Sacer*, II, 2). Translated by Lorenzo Chiesa and Matteo Mandarini. Stanford: Stanford University Press, 2011.

LD   *Language and Death: The Place of Negativity*. Translated by Karen E. Pinkus and Michael Hardt. Minneapolis: University of Minnesota Press, 1991.

MC   *The Man Without Content*. Translated by Georgia Albert. Stanford: Stanford University Press, 1999.

ME   *Means Without End: Notes on Politics*. Translated by Vincenzo Binetti and Cesare Casarino. Minneapolis: University of Minnesota Press, 2000.

N   *Nudities*. Translated by David Kishik and Stefan Pedatella. Stanford: Stanford University Press, 2010.

O   *The Open: Man and Animal*. Translated by Kevin Attell. Stanford: Stanford University Press, 2004.

P   *Profanations*. Translated by Jeff Fort. New York: Zone Books, 2007.

PC   *Potentialities: Collected Essays in Philosophy*. Edited and translated by Daniel Heller-Roazen. Stanford: Stanford University Press, 1999.

RA   *Remnants of Auschwitz: The Witness and the Archive* (*Homo Sacer*, III). Translated by Daniel Heller-Roazen. New York: Zone Books, 2000.

S   *Stanzas: Word and Phantasm in Western Culture*. Translated by Ronald L. Martinez. Minneapolis: University of Minnesota Press, 1993.

SE   *State of Exception* (*Homo Sacer*, II, 1). Translated by Kevin Attell. Chicago: University of Chicago Press, 2005.

SL   *The Sacrament of Language: An Archeology of the Oath* (*Homo Sacer*, II, 3). Translated by Adam Kotsko. Stanford: Stanford University Press, 2010.

ST   *The Signature of All Things: On Method*. Translated by Luca D'Isanto and Kevin Attell. New York: Zone Books, 2009.

TR   *The Time That Remains: A Commentary on the Letter to the Romans*. Translated by Patricia Dailey. Stanford: Stanford University Press, 2005.

WA   *What Is an Apparatus? and Other Essays*. Translated by David Kishik and Stefan Pedatella. Stanford: Stanford University Press, 2009.

The Power of Life

Introduction

LIFE IN VENICE

The Philosophical Subject

The year 1968 was a remarkable one in the life of Giorgio Agamben. It began with a trip to Athens, his first visit to the ruins of the birthplace of Western philosophy and politics—the main planes in between which his thought still oscillates. Then, in May, he left for Paris to take part in the final chain of events that turned the city on its head during that restless spring. From Paris he went to New York. After attending a performance of *Hair* on Broadway, he took the train up to Harvard, where he participated in the International Seminar, a gathering of young intellectuals from around the world, headed by Professor Henry Kissinger. The director, however, was rarely to be seen, so the days passed with the seminar's host, a young philosophy professor named Stanley Cavell, usually showing the participants old Hollywood movies in between discussions about American culture. One day, Kissinger actually gave a short talk. At its end, Agamben, then twenty-six years old, raised his hand and frankly told the lecturer that he understood nothing about politics. Kissinger, according to Agamben, did not respond but only smirked. Not long after he returned home to Rome, Agamben packed his suitcase once again and checked into a small hotel in Provence, where he again participated in a seminar, this time with Martin Heidegger (another professor with a dubious political involvement). It was this event that initiated him into the world of philosophy for good. Agamben recollects: "At Le Thor, Heidegger held his seminar in a garden shaded by tall trees. At times, however, we left the village, walking in the direction of Thouzon or Rebanquet, and the seminar then took place in front of a small hut hidden away in the midst of an olive grove. One day, when the seminar neared its end and the students crowded round him, pressing him with questions, Heidegger merely remarked: 'You can see my limit; I can't'" (*IP*, 59).

The stamps on Agamben's passport from this eventful year include some of the central stations in what would become his elaborate intellectual itinerary while traveling through the Western tradition. But they also help us comprehend the very limit that Heidegger claims he is unable to see. One way to interpret Heidegger's blindness, which has guided (or haunted) Agamben ever since, is to say that there is a certain concept, proposition, thesis, or argument that the philosopher cannot comprehend and that his followers need to try to articulate. "Until you understand a writer's ignorance," Coleridge declares, "presume yourself ignorant of his understanding."[1] Like the human eye, every thinker has a lacuna, which can be compensated for in two ways: either through constant movement (the thought, like the eye, must always change its position, so with the help of our short-term memory the blind spot can be erased) or by the employment of another perspective (even though another thinker, like a second eye, has a blind spot exactly as the first one does, using them together enables us to have an unobstructed view of the matter at hand). Yet another way to treat Heidegger's claim is to simply rewrite it thus: "Perhaps you could see my limit if you could see my self, but I can't." This is, more or less, what Ludwig Wittgenstein had in mind when he wrote that the subject, which he also called "the philosophical I," is "the limit—not a part of the world."[2] My "I" is missing from my world in the same way that my eye is missing from its visual field. Though human beings seem to have what Heidegger took to be a reflexive ability to be concerned about their very being, they also tend to relapse into Ovid's predicament, as they live and know not that they live. We always operate in the tension between this gnosis and ignorance. The Platonic injunction to "know thyself" is nice counsel but never an accomplished fact. From this perspective, we could suggest that the focal point, which is also the lacuna of every thinker, or the horizon, which is also the threshold of his or her thought, is his or her self. But this is a very special kind of self that has nothing to do with any individual, personal, psychological, or physiological considerations. Wittgenstein's philosophical "I" (or the

"I" of the philosopher) is, rather, a descendant of Kant's transcendental "I" and an ancestor of "the new postconscious and postsubjective, impersonal and non-individual transcendental field" that Agamben, following Gilles Deleuze, calls "*a life*" (*PC*, 225). When a person moves in this (admittedly still very vague) direction, his individuality could be said to become, in Walter Benjamin's words, "secondary to his life just as a flower's is to its perfume, or a star's to its light."[3]

The rumor about "the death of the author" has been greatly exaggerated. Put differently, though no less facetiously, a good author is not necessarily a dead author. In Agamben's philosophy, authors still enjoy a rather sweet afterlife, even if, in the wake of Roland Barthes and Michel Foucault, they are no longer considered to be entities that stand behind, are expressed in, or are represented by their work, and even though they lack a definable presence that can be located or captured. Instead, he claims that the life of the author is "put into play" within the work itself, in such a way that the author is transformed within the text into a "gesture," which is the name Agamben gives to "that which remains unexpressed in each expressive act" (*P*, 66–67). There is no apparent reason why we should not apply this approach to the very author to which this book is dedicated, by treating his own life as a gesture in language, so to speak, rather than as a mere fact in the world. This enables us to understand a critical point: Agamben's work is "not a *writing*, but a *form of life*," as he suggests in a different context (*TR*, 122). In other words, although this book is dedicated to Agamben's *philosophy* of life, its success or failure may be measured by its ability to lead the reader to imagine a *form* of life, by its capacity to clarify how his way of thinking points toward a way of living. Scholars tend to devote their research to a single thinker, rather than a single subject, either because they feel the need to scrutinize the internal coherence of the thought or because they are dazzled by it. But is it also possible to take a similar route in order to try to illuminate *a life*? Can the subject of philosophy be the philosophical subject? If Robert Musil's claim that one needs "to live as one reads" has more than a merely aesthetic appeal, then what is the ethical, even political relationship between reading and living?[4]

The problem, however, is that it is not difficult to get the impression that Agamben "let the wick of his life be consumed completely by the gentle flame" of his work, to use another one of Benjamin's beautiful formulations.[5] But the truth of the matter is that neither Agamben's "life" nor his "work" can really make a lot of sense independently of one another, because they both operate in the zone of indetermination that we call a "lifework," which is all but extinct in the intellectual climate of our day. Since he always effaces "himself" by speaking through proxies, since he only asserts "his own philosophy" by means of synthesizing the writings of others, Agamben seems to follow Socrates's basic insistence that he does not give birth to his own ideas but only engenders them in his interlocutors. (One apparent difference, it must be said, is that for Agamben it is typically old texts, rather than young boys, that are pregnant with new and radical thoughts.) Despite these hurdles, this book will show how the true power of Agamben's work lies in its ability to reimagine political action, philosophical thought, and the ethical subject in such a way that the three constitute the corners of a triangle whose center is called "form of life."

There Is Something Inside the Text

To demonstrate how this book directs itself toward the very axis on which Agamben's thought turns, let us take a look at *"Experimentum linguae."* Written in the late 1980s, this essay marks a subtle yet decisive turn that efficiently divides his writings into what may be called the "early Agamben" and the "later Agamben." In this threshold text he articulates in unequivocal terms "the terrain toward which all my work is oriented," which comes down to the following questions: "What is the meaning of 'there is language'; what is the meaning of 'I speak'?" (*IH,* 6). There is, however, something rather suspicious about this too easily granted confession. Retrospectively, the attentive reader can see that this self-conscious moment marks a genuine watershed in Agamben's work rather than the place in which he comes to terms with it once and for all. The point insisted on most fervently in a thinker's work is often the point seen least clearly; or, in Agamben's own words, "only a thought that does not conceal its own unsaid—but constantly takes it up and elaborates it—may eventually lay claim to originality" (*ST*, 8). How, after all, can one express the very existence of language, the recently discovered center (or transfixion) of Agamben's thought? It is surely impossible to formulate a sentence *in* language that can express the existence of language as such. In the last lines of his essay, Agamben admits that there is only one possible way to express the fact that I speak: *that I live.* The existence of life is the proper manifestation for the existence of language. The result, therefore, of the experiment conducted in Agamben's essay, or the experience it tries to evoke, transports his thought from the question of language to the question of life. It is human life, understood "as *ethos*, as ethical way," as form of life (which is also nothing but an experiment/experience), that will function from this point on as the core of his entire philosophy (*IH*, 9–10). Even though the notions of language and life both play pivotal roles in his work from beginning to (the yet-to-be-seen) end, his thought's center of gravity seems to shift here from the former to the latter.

This does not mean that after his "turn" Agamben will hold that language simply dwells in life, that the lived has priority over the said. Such ideas inform the genre of biography: this effort to write a life, to dictate a form of life, as it were. Writing a biography about the life of a writer, for example, is mainly an attempt to reconstruct, explain, or justify the written work on the basis of the lived experience. One of the problems, however, with the lives of thinkers is that no matter how extraordinary their story may be, they tend to pursue an undistinguished life on paper. Even our cultish fascination with figures like Kafka and Benjamin does not arise from their life story per se but from this tension between their "vital" failures and their eventual "linguistic" triumphs. This is what stands behind Heidegger's apparent contempt toward any attempt to speak about the historical and personal context of a philosophical thought, which he famously dismissed by saying, "Aristotle was born, worked, and died."[6]

Agamben's resistance to the biographical temptation does not lead him to ignore life altogether by claiming that "there is nothing outside the text."

Instead, he presents, before and after his ostensible turn, the link between language and life in a manner diametrically opposite to that of the biographer. He maintains that *"life is only what is made in speech,"* that life is essentially nothing but a "fable" (*EP*, 81). Originating from the prologue to Saint John's Gospel, where life is said to dwell in the Word, this decisive idea found its exemplary manifestation in the medieval tradition of love poetry that extends from the troubadours to the Dolce stil Novo and, most important, to Dante Alighieri. On the face of it, these poems are the direct result of the existence of a certain flesh-and-blood woman with whom the poet fell in love. The biographer is therefore tempted to look for the thirteenth-century Florentine girl that Dante refers to in his *Vita nuova* as "Beatrice." Agamben questions this practice by claiming that any biographical event that the poem seems to put into words must be considered as invented, as fabulated. In his view, what is poeticized has a decisive priority over what is lived. Dante's true love, Agamben argues, is actually directed toward *language itself,* for which the poeticized Beatrice stands as the supreme metaphor. After all, it is only from this "event of language"—a poem written in the vernacular—that Dante's "new life" could emerge (*EP*, 58). This realization needs to inform any attempt, including the present one, to think about the ordinarily uneventful life of the philosopher; otherwise, it is doomed to fall into the double trap of biography and hagiography. Hannah Arendt sums up this attitude in her elucidation of Heidegger's one-line biography of Aristotle: "We are so accustomed to the old opposition of reason versus passion, spirit versus life, that the idea of a *passionate* thinking, in which thinking and aliveness become one, takes us somewhat aback."[7] There is a certain passion in Agamben's thought; there is a life that appears to be embedded in his words. This, before anything else, is what his reader should not lose sight of.

Agamben often thinks about language as pure potentiality: not merely as the communication of this or that piece of information but, above all, as communicability itself. What is really important for him is not that we speak about all sorts of things but that we have this capacity to speak, *speakability* as such. Language is a power that may *or may not* be exercised, and it is the second point—what we *can not* say (which is not the same as what we *cannot* say)—on which he never tires of insisting. Nevertheless, it is impossible to even imagine the existence of this power of language apart from what we will call from now on "the power of life," without accounting for the living being who prefers or prefers not to speak, or act, or even think. The world may be filled with mountains of white paper and oceans of black ink, but without at least a single scribe (but also at least the hope of an addressee) nothing would ever be written. The potentiality of language is therefore not to be conflated with what Ferdinand de Saussure calls *langue*, which is language's abstract structure independent of its utterance in actual speech (*parole*). As Saussure himself conceded, there can be no science of language that does not study "the life of signs in the domain of social life."[8] If we forget for a second that language is always embedded in shared human praxis, that words are simply patterns in the weave of our common lives, then we might mistakenly believe, as Agamben himself once did, that "the power of language must be directed toward language," that "the eye must see its blind spot," which is, of course, impossible: "If I were truly able to see the blind spot in my eye," he admits in almost the same breath, "I would see nothing" (*IP*, 99, 128). Yet again, a proven method for coping with such a lacuna is to employ another eye, another thought, another thinker. It is only in Wittgenstein's work that a radical philosophy of language becomes inextricable from a new philosophy of life, where it becomes clear that "to imagine a language means to imagine a form of life."[9] But even though the relationship between life and language finds its most potent expression in Wittgenstein, he still fails to see as clearly as Agamben does the *political* significance of both. This relationship between politics and life is the central concern of this book.

Nonparticipation

By the time Agamben was a teenager, the scorching traces of the Second World War, during which he was only an infant, were virtually imperceptible in the unabashed bustle of Rome. His formative years coincide with the short-lived cultural and economic renaissance that the city experienced between the collapse of the Fascist regime in the mid-1940s and the spread of its corrupt politics in the mid-1970s. Because his father operated a movie theater, Agamben saw many films as a child, sometimes even two in a single day. But there were also many books in the Agambens' household, some of them works of philosophy, and they constituted the first items in what would become the mammoth reading list that shaped his mature thought. Sitting in his small apartment in Venice, which can be reached after climbing a rather steep set of stairs, he said that before his mother passed away, she gave him a piece of paper that she had saved since the time he was seven years old. "It was all there!" he said with astonishment. On this page, Agamben claimed, was a condensed version of his entire mature philosophy. As for its content, he remained mute.

After familiarizing himself with the required classical languages and literature taught at school, he managed to complete a first degree with a concentration in law before losing faith in formal education, which he still deems, at least in his case, worthless. It was instead the intelligentsia's demimonde outside the dogmatic bounds of academia that formed his subsequent career. Living in Rome, Paris, and London, he moved in various circles, befriending writers such as Elsa Morante and Italo Calvino, poets such as Ingeborg Bachmann and José Bergamin, philosophers such as Jacques Derrida and Jean-Luc Nancy, and radical intellectuals–turned–filmmakers such as Pier Paolo Pasolini and Guy Debord. But more important, it was his immersion in the writings of a swelling number of (mostly dead) authors, together with his ability to spin them within his own studies into an intricate web of references, that gave his work its distinct charm. It is quite surprising to realize that the eerie breadth of his erudition comes from the mind of an almost complete autodidact. This fact became clearer during a midday walk through the streets of Venice. "Look at these buildings," he said while stopping in a typical piazza; "none of them were built by professional architects." One of the easier arguments to make is that modern structures, those Corbusian "machines for living" produced by university-trained architects, are palpable eyesores when placed next to the (essentially objective) beauty of Venice. But isn't it also possible, in light of Agamben's work, to make a similar argument concerning many of the texts produced by "professional" philosophers these days?

When Agamben came upon Arendt's writings in the late 1960s, he was so thrilled to discover their sense of promise and urgency that he sent her a personal note expressing his gratitude. But as the events of the 1960s subsided, as Arendt's work was somewhat forgotten and generally dismissed by the professional naysayers, the air of possibility was replaced by that of a missed opportunity. The fact that some years after her death she was admitted into the philosophical pantheon through an endless parade of conferences and monographs does not change much, as the opportunity to act upon the thought was missed for the sake of opportunism. In other words, something that could have happened did not take place.[10] At the turn of the new millennium, it was suddenly Agamben's name that was whispered in knowing circles around the globe with a sense of exigency. But the lessons of the past make it clear that the potency of this new way of thinking will have to face enormous, perhaps insurmountable, obstacles (starting with those mounted by a new generation of professional naysayers) before it can somehow imprint itself on our way of living. In this spirit, Agamben laments in an essay from the mid-1970s that our age "is not the epoch of faith and not even the epoch of incredulity," but rather "it is more than anything else the epoch of bad faith" in which "the first duty of each intellectual must consist in the nonparticipation in this lie."[11]

It is easy to assume and pretentious to assert that, unlike any other human activity, philosophy exists in some sort of eternal vacuum. Ignoring the academic context in which theoretical work is done today is like disregarding unsustainable practices that upset our faltering ecological system. The notion that the campus is a hotbed for revolt is a common myth that does not take into account the usual passivity and dispassion that prevails in classrooms and during faculty office hours around the world. Remember that even in the 1960s, when student unrest shook the foundations of entire cities and states, one of the protestors' main targets was the academic apparatus itself. The reason is that the college was never meant to perpetuate the revolutionary desires of the young generation but rather to block them, or to channel those desires into so-called productive (read "futile") avenues. Even if deviation is allowed, it is circumscribed to specific times and places, or exceptions, that never interfere with the overall rule of the status quo. The teaching and writing of the professor are not really meant to agitate anyone, as radical creativity is transformed into timid and monotonous production. To some extent, the cherished academic freedom, much like the coveted tenure position, is nothing but the sleeping pill of comfortable living. Today, it becomes increasingly obvious that forms of resistance rarely converge with forms of academic discourse, which is not infrequently fueled by bad faith. When one realizes that the main agenda behind the demonstrations of the current student body is to protect its own privileges and those of its professors, one knows that something has gone terribly amiss. But even though it is not easy to see how the hegemony of the university-factory could be effectively contested, Agamben's lifework still offers a viable model for a kind of nonparticipatory participation in the operation of this sprawling, monopolistic institution.

The Mirror of Narcissus

He is tall and lean, with a slight hunch that seems to register years of lucubration at his desk. On first impression, his narrow eyes and fixed gaze may appear predatory, but after a while his taciturn demeanor gives his interlocutor the impression that his main strategy of attack is to refrain from doing so. Though his books may lead one to assume that his thoughts wander in a thousand different directions, in person he tends to be very calculated. As much as he seems to be receptive to everything, he can also be quite unyielding. "Protect your heart with all vigilance, for it is the wellspring of life"—this passage from Proverbs 4:23, which was inscribed above the entrance to Heidegger's home, also informs Agamben's comportment quite efficiently. One evening after a conversation that made this matter clear enough, he proposed that we go to a small bar along one of the canals where a young American folk singer was about to give an informal concert. After the show the singer was introduced to the philosopher and straightaway posed to him the first question that most people associate with his strange vocation: "So how should I live my life?" Agamben answered right away: "Probably the way you live it." It was a reassuring reply, but the word "probably" lingered in the air of the night longer than expected.

Agamben's relationship with art and artists is very instructive for those interested in the way he sees his own thought and the thinker "behind" it. At the beginning of his philosophical work, in the first pages of *The Man Without Content*, his reader encounters an emphatic plea for the inseparability of art from life. Developing Nietzsche's critique of disinterested beauty, Agamben takes to task the Kantian aestheticization of art, which leads to an emphasis on the spectator's sensation at the expense of the artist's creation. Agamben reminds us that it is the immediate, inspired hand, more than the distant, judging eye, that has the most intimate relationship with the work of art. Pygmalion, "the sculptor who becomes so enamored of his creation as to wish that it belonged no longer to art but to life," is the symbol of Agamben's vision (*MC*, 2). Arthur Rimbaud and Rainer Maria Rilke, who insist that poetry must "change life," are his obvious models. The ultimate concern of such a vision is a promise of happiness instead of only a spectacle of happiness; its aim is the good life rather than good taste. This position offers a surprising take on the received view of Plato's infamous "crusade" against the poets who endanger the city-state. This position rings so wrong in our modern ears only because art does not have the same influence on us as it did on him: "Only because art has left the sphere of *interest* to become merely *interesting*," Agamben writes, "do we welcome it so warmly" (*MC*, 4). The decline of censorship, he implies, is not so much the result of a growing liberal tolerance as an indication that the artwork in question is impotent, since no one cares about banning ineffective art. Though he does not yet employ the word, it is obvious that art is understood here within a *political* context. As improbable as it may sound, from this standpoint beauty is conceived as an "indescribably more ruthless and cruel upheaval than any political revolution ever was," as Musil writes in *The Man Without Qualities*, to which Agamben alludes in the title of his first book.[12] A similar argument is shared by Benjamin, who asks us to combat the "aestheticizing of politics" through the "politicization of art," which can be achieved even without dedicating the artwork to an explicitly political subject matter.[13] Given the current tendency of art as well as philosophy to transform themselves into mere spectacles— their "museification" or "academization"—it is not easy to remember this almost always unfulfilled promise that both of these fields of action can also function as potent forms of insurgency. It is also not hard to forget that a work of philosophy can be a work of beauty, too.

In the mid-1970s Agamben spent a very significant and productive year doing research at the Warburg Library in London. Aby Warburg is generally considered to be an art historian, but his work tends to resist the usual aestheticization of art that Agamben criticizes in his first book, and thus to cast aside the basic attitude of his discipline. "It is as if," Agamben comments, "Warburg were interested in this discipline solely to place within it the seed that would cause it to explode" (PC, 90). That this observation could also apply to Agamben's own volatile relationship with the discipline of philosophy is no coincidence. Warburg's great unfinished project best exemplifies his unique approach: in the last years of his life, he composed an atlas of images arranged according to various iconographical themes, where one can easily find a medieval drawing placed next to a modern advertisement photo. He called his project "Mnemosyne," after the Greek goddess of memory (and the mother of the Muses). In opposition to some critics, Agamben claims that Warburg's final project is neither capricious nor banal and insists that this atlas "was not an iconographical repertory but something like a mirror of Narcissus," by which Agamben means that it was essentially created in Warburg's image, according to his likeness (PC, 102). Like Narcissus, who looked into the pond only to see his own reflection, what one sees when one searches through "Mnemosyne" is not necessarily Warburg's personality but rather what F. Scott Fitzgerald calls a "personage," which is the sort of man who always "gathers," who "is never thought apart from what he's done," since a personage, unlike a personality, is "a bar on which a thousand things have been hung."[14] Such a personage is not far from what Agamben calls "the man without content." The work of this man, his life, is in this sense a work of art, though it would be futile to search here for the artist behind the work or to confuse this man with either the aesthete or the dandy. In 1975, when Agamben developed this line of thought in "Warburg and the Nameless Science," he saw his essay "as the first of a series of portraits dedicated to exemplary personalities, each of which was to represent a human science" (*PC*, 101). In 2001, Agamben still believed that this planned book of profiles would eventually become the final installment of his *Homo Sacer* project, to be dedicated to the notion of form of life. Today, it is not clear that this book will ever be written in its intended form. But what *is* clear is that the lesson from Warburg's work could still be applied to Agamben's own sprawling oeuvre—his very own Narcissus's pond—in its ability to reflect not just a philosophy but also a life of a man without content. As is the case with Andy Warhol, if you want to know all about Giorgio Agamben, just look at the surface of his books and essays and seminars, and there he is. There is nothing behind it.

The Specter of Venice

From time to time Agamben allows himself to add a subtle personal touch to his texts. An interesting recent example is "On the Uses and Disadvantages of Living Among Specters," in which he contemplates his life in Venice. If, as Wittgenstein once suggested, language can be compared to a city, then Venice, according to Agamben, is like a dead language. Living in Venice, he claims, is like studying Latin. Though it is possible to read and even speak Latin with great effort and the help of a dictionary, it is still impossible, or nearly impossible, to find in this dead language the place of a subject, of the speaker who says "I." This leads him to describe Venice as a spectral city inhabited by ghosts. Perhaps, his argument continues, Venice is an emblem for much of our modern world, where cities and languages, peoples and states, religious orders and secular institutions, could be said to be essentially dead, although everyone continues to *pretend* that they are not, to treat them *as if* they were still alive. It is much easier to come to terms with the fact that eventually I am going to die, to achieve what Heidegger calls a "being-toward-death," than to face the fact that *I am already dead*, which is the reason that ghosts are often depicted as being consumed by quantities of angst that would probably crush the soul of any living human being. "For a man can never be in death," Saint Augustine writes, "in a worse sense than where death itself is without death."[15] Nevertheless, there are also those special ghosts that learn to accept their ghostliness, because they realize, together with Agamben, that "spectrality is a form of life; a posthumous or complementary life that begins only when everything is finished. Spectrality has, with respect to life, the incomparable grace and astuteness of that which has been completed, the courtesy and precision of those who no longer have anything ahead of them" (*N*, 39).

Another appealing aspect of the spectral form of life is that ghosts rarely follow a leader, whether political or spiritual, nor do they tend to lead others. "There is no Virgil to guide us in this Inferno," reads a graffito in Agamben's neighborhood, which he took a visitor to see with what could have been a gesture of self-effacement. (When the spray-painted letters began to fade away, they were reinforced by Agamben's friend, who then added a small stenciled image of a Banksy-like rat in the bottom-right corner.) The specter of Venice continued to walk in the virtually empty streets one evening in late November. Since nightlife is somewhat limited in that city, it is not so difficult to imagine, a few hours after dinnertime, that it is, indeed, a ghost town. This impression was especially strong on that particular evening, as the rain sent the last tourists back into their hotel rooms. Agamben predicted that the next day at dawn the water would rise and flood the city (an increasingly recurring phenomenon that forewarns of the day the city will be completely submerged by the lagoon). Though he said that Venice feels like home, especially whenever he returns from abroad, he also admitted that it is the place, more than the people, that he really feels close to. This is perhaps why his nocturnal *flâneries* in the desolate streets are one of his most cherished pastimes. Toward the end of the stroll he pointed at the Dogana in the distance, with its twin statues of Atlas carrying the globe on which Fortuna is standing. It reminded him of the final scene from Debord's last film, *In girum imus nocte et consumimur igni* ("We go wandering at night, consumed by fire," an old Latin palindrome of whose origins Agamben remains uncertain). The leitmotif of this semiautobiographical film is a slow traveling shot of Venice taken from a moving motorboat. The last of these scenes happens at the very end of the movie, as Debord's voice is heard in the background: "In any case," he says, "one traverses an era as one passes the Dogana promontory—that is to say, rather quickly."[16]

Dialectic of Endarkenment

Darkness Visible

"Let there be darkness": it is hard to resist placing these words in the opening chapter of a book dedicated to Agamben's philosophy of life. "Light," he writes, "is only the coming to itself of the dark" (*IP*, 119). There seems to be little hope in his mind that light really has the capacity to enlighten. A light can only flicker, like a distant star, and the darkness that surrounds it is not meant to understand it. In fact, even the "total darkness" of the nightly sky is for him "the testimony of a time in which the stars did not yet shine" (*RA*, 162). Even Arendt's Gnostic faith in the power of singular bright "men in dark times" to ever more slightly make a difference in this world does not seem to play the same role in Agamben's thought. Be that as it may, he also appears to be possessed by an exigent demand to which he cannot not answer: it is difficult to miss (though many still do) that there is a constant attempt throughout his writings to bear witness to a certain light or, at least, to a glimmer. If you have ever tried to catch fireflies with your hand on a hot summer night, you may have experienced this curious philosophical comportment. Call it, if you wish, a dialectic of *endarkenment*, by which I mean a perpetual attempt "to perceive, in the darkness of the present, this light that strives to reach us but cannot" (*WA*, 46).

Consider, for example, the *Homo Sacer* series of books, Agamben's major contribution to the field of political philosophy, and compare it with *The Republic*, the founding text in this tradition. The most famous image in Plato's book is of a prisoner who is released from his chains to face the sunlight of truth, of this gloomy cave from which the reader is supposed to emerge with a little help from the philosopher. In Agamben's work, the experience seems to be the reverse: in the middle of life, while sitting on a comfortable chair with a lamp and maybe even a hot drink in a reasonably secure corner of the earth, the reader suddenly finds herself in a dark forest. This experience echoes not only the first lines of Dante's *Inferno* but also the opening scene of Kafka's *The Trial*, where Joseph K., the protagonist of the story, wakes up one morning to discover that he is charged in a shadowy court of committing an unspecified crime. Our life, with its basic rights and liberties, is usually protected by the laws of a state; but it can also easily be transformed into what Agamben calls a bare or naked life, which is stripped of its way or form of life. With a blink of an eye, a flick of a pen, or a press of a button, any "good citizen" from any "respected country" (it does not matter whether it is democratic or not) can be excluded from the state-run "protection plan" and thus be exposed to random acts of violence. Even as we live our seemingly meaningful and civil everyday lives, we should not forget that, from the perspective of the powers that be, we may very well be perceived as no more than a mere fact, a docile body, or a simple number, which can and should be governed, monitored, disciplined, and controlled. Agamben thus observes that "in the eyes of authority—and maybe rightly so—nothing looks more like a terrorist than the ordinary man" (*WA*, 23).

But what at first appears to the human eye as pitch dark—similar to what, in the initial ascension from the cave, appears to Plato's prisoner as the blinding light of the sun—simply takes time to adjust to. You will certainly begin to discern your surroundings after spending a few seconds in an unlit room, even though objects may still look monochromatic (as Agamben's work might seem at times). What you then see, however, is "no light; but rather darkness visible," to echo Milton's *Paradise Lost*.[1] We therefore need to find a way to cope with the shadows inside the cave that Plato deems to be mere appearances in a time when the burning sun—understood here not only as a metaphor for absolute truth or God but also for the absolute king or sovereign—is possibly undergoing an eclipse. This, however, does not mean that we now have no choice but to live in a relativistic or anarchic chaos, as some nihilistic readings of the allegory of the cave may lead one to assume. "Because human beings neither are nor have to be any essence, any nature, or any specific destiny," Agamben writes, "their condition is the most empty and the most insubstantial of all: it is the truth. What remains hidden from them is not something behind appearance, but rather appearing itself. . . . The task of politics is to return appearance itself to appearance, to cause appearance itself to appear" (*ME*, 94–95).

In this way, Agamben reveals the intimate relationship between the prisoner in Plato's *Republic* and the bat from Aristotle's *Metaphysics*: both are blinded by the blazing light of the sun, and thus they are comparable symbols of the great difficulty that humans have in comprehending "the things which are by nature most evident of all," because this kind of difficulty, Aristotle claims, "does not lie in the things, but in us."[2] For Agamben, however, it is not light but rather darkness that is visible, that is apparent. Nevertheless, we still face it as if we were bats in daylight, which is understandable, given that for so long we were told that the sun is supposed to be good for us. The difficulty of seeing this visible darkness lies not in the things but in us, in our failure to see what is right under our nose. So maybe behind what we like to think of as a romantic cliché stands a simple realization: only during sunset, when our shadows grow much longer than our selves, can we begin to appear to one another; only at twilight can we begin to see each other's truth.

Biopolitics in Miniature

Agamben's strategy postulates that the first text in political thought demanding our undistracted attention is not *The Republic* but *Leviathan*, which places his analysis within a decidedly modern context. One of the best ways to approach Hobbes's imposing tomb of a book is to simply inspect its frontispiece, as Agamben did in a lecture in New York during the tumultuous fall semester of 2001. It is worthwhile to examine this engraving quite closely, since it can not only offer a window into Hobbes's system but also encapsulate a miniature model of Agamben's extensive critique of modern politics. Nevertheless, like all miniatures, what follows is not going to be an adequate substitution for the real thing. This section is meant only to serve as a quick and idiosyncratic primer for the five books that constitute (so far) the *Homo Sacer* project. This chapter as a whole introduces some of the most basic elements of the political and philosophical "darkness" as Agamben understands it. On this background, we will also begin to glimpse some possible illuminations.

Observe the great leviathan, "that mortal God," on the top half of Hobbes's frontispiece, which is represented as a disproportionally large sovereign with a majestic crown.[3] This giant dominates the image even though it is placed behind a stretch of hills, leaving to your imagination the shape of its lower body. Given the title of the book—the Hebrew name for a mystical sea monster—it could very well be a fishtail submerged in the sea. Or perhaps it is a puppet maneuvered by an invisible hand. Speculation aside, it is the upper body to which our attention is drawn. The arms and torso of the giant are composed of a multitude of little people. The body politic, the citizens, constitute the very body of the sovereign. The people's backs are turned to the viewer, since the collective attention of the commonwealth is focused on the head, on their leader. As one can expect, the people are excluded from this head (of state). A standard reading of *Leviathan* establishes a bipolar opposition between the state of nature (where "man is a wolf to man," since life is "solitary, poor, nasty, brutish, and short") and the political state (where you transfer the right to govern yourself to the sovereign, who thereafter has the exclusive power to protect the citizenry from any harm).[4] In a move that we will witness time and again throughout Agamben's work, he questions this clear-cut separation by tracing the sovereign's special position within this scheme. Notice that in the engraving he is located far away from the city, beyond a valley and behind the hills. The ruler, who at first glance appears to be the pinnacle of the political state, actually remains in a sort of natural state, outside the city, and therefore stands as the exception to the rule. In the first volume of *Homo Sacer*, subtitled *Sovereign Power and Bare Life*, Agamben explains: "This is why in Hobbes, the foundation of sovereign power is to be sought not in the subjects' free renunciation of their natural right but in the sovereign's preservation of his natural right to do anything to anyone" (*HS*, 106). The basic mistake of the standard reading of *Leviathan* lies therefore in looking at the situation from the fixed position given to the one viewing the frontispiece, which is the vantage point of the populace. Notice that when you place the picture close to your nose while focusing on the monarch with his outstretched arms, the vista is quite similar to what you would see if you still bother to participate in those political assemblies at the city square: a multitude of backs, and a single head elevated above the rest. By means of your gaze, you become one with this commonwealth that voices in unison its support or demands, its hopes or fears, and you are led to believe that this is the meaning of the political. Agamben's discovery lies in renouncing this perspective and assuming instead the viewpoint of the sovereign, for whom the city does not appear as bustling with life but as if it were dissolved: "Contrary to our modern habit of representing the political realm in terms of citizens' rights, free will, and social contracts, from the point of view of sovereignty *only bare life is authentically political*" (*HS*, 106). This shift in the reader's perspective produces an effect similar to that of an X-ray: what traditionally looks like a normal human being transforms into a ghostly white skeleton on a thick dark background. The "political animal" that Aristotle saw in man is reduced to just another animal. More than a century before Agamben, Nietzsche had already described this perilous condition in unambiguous terms: "State, where the slow suicide of all is called 'life.'"[5]

Let us focus now on a place that the commonwealth cannot see because its collective back is turned away. Here, on the bottom of the top half (or the center) of the frontispiece, one can detect a small city surrounded by a wall. But the city is nearly empty: except for a few almost indiscernible little soldiers bearing arms, there are only buildings and desolate streets. The city appears as if it were in the midst of some kind of state of emergency and therefore was put under curfew. The traditional picture of politics as a public sphere suffused with words and deeds is nowhere to be found. In the eyes of the sovereign, the war of all against all cannot be fully distinguished—temporally, spatially, or conceptually—from the more or less peaceful, civilized, and protected society in which we *think* that we live. The citizens may believe that the state of nature is in every sense "behind them," but from the sovereign's viewpoint it persists as "the exception and the threshold that constitutes and dwells within" the seemingly lawful and normal state (*HS*, 106). In *State of Exception*, the next volume in the *Homo Sacer* series, Agamben focuses on a specific apparatus that is deployed whenever an emergency situation is declared in our modern nation-states: by virtue of a special clause in the law itself, there is always the possibility of suspending certain laws and rights, thus giving the sovereign and his assistants unrestrained power to, indeed, "do anything to anyone." In this state of exception, the individuals that come together to compose the Hobbesian commonwealth may no longer be protected by the law that is usually meant to keep them out of harm's way. In the final analysis, they are marked not by their capacity to speak and act but by the capacity of their bodies to be *killed* with impunity. This, Agamben boldly claims, is "the new political body of the West," which is perfectly illustrated in another version of the frontispiece that Hobbes commissioned for a special parchment copy of *Leviathan*, dedicated to Charles II.[6] The startling difference is that here, in an image meant for the exclusive gaze of the sovereign, the people that compose the giant's body are looking straight at the viewer rather than turning their backs away, and the expressions on their faces are evidently full of dread. They no longer look like respectable citizens but like what Agamben calls *homines sacri*, sacred men, who are ready for the massacre. According to this analysis, the killing of *homo sacer* is considered neither as homicide nor as sacrifice, since it is banished to a space that lies outside both human and divine law. Politics thus transforms into *biopolitics*: the political power over the bare lives of those sacred men, women, and children.

This, however, is not the end of the story. In *On the Citizen*, the first systematic formulation of his political thought, Hobbes makes an interesting though rarely noticed distinction "between the *right* and the *exercise* of sovereign power" by comparing the government of this or that commonwealth to the government of the world en masse: "When he who has the right to reign wishes to participate himself in all judgments, consolations, and public actions, it is a way of running things comparable to God's attending directly to everything himself, contrary to the order of nature."[7] Agamben uses this quote as an epigraph for the next part of *Homo Sacer*, titled *The Kingdom and the Glory*. To illustrate this point, notice that in the familiar engraving for Hobbes's *Leviathan* the sovereign holds a sword in one hand and a staff in the other, which are conventionally interpreted as representations of the earthly (political) and heavenly (theological) powers, respectively. But since his arms and torso are made of people, those powers can be said to be, both figuratively and literally, in the hands of the people. The sovereign is therefore said to reign, but he does not govern. The day-to-day governance of the modern state is entrusted to the bureaucracy, exactly as, in medieval theology, the actual governance of the world is entrusted to the angels. What, then, is the function of God and the sovereign within their respective theological and political economies? What is left for them to do? Agamben explains that since the sovereign, like God, has no practical role in government, he can only idly bask in his own glory (given to him, of course, by the multitude). The sword and the staff from the frontispiece may therefore also symbolize the power and the glory of the mortal as well as the immortal gods. This interpretation of the image may be well and good, until one notices that Agamben places at the beginning of his own book a different frontispiece that is a direct reply to Hobbes's. It is a common medieval representation of the heavenly throne, the seat of divine power, complete with all its necessary symbols and regalia. Only one element is missing: God is absent, the seat vacant. "The empty throne" is the emblem of Agamben's assertion that at the center of the governmental machine there is *nothing*. But this, of course, is already present in a larval form in Hobbes's original frontispiece: under the real crown, in between the physical sword and staff, above the vividly drawn city, this giant creature without fear is actually a specter devoid of life. The sovereign, after all, is not a real man but an artificial one, like the Jewish golem that was created only to serve in the rabbi's household but then grew larger and larger until it overcame its own master. (According to the lore, the only way to get rid of this golem is to climb up to its forehead, where the word *emet*, "truth" in Hebrew, was first written in order to give life to the dummy. You must then erase the first letter, the privative *aleph*, thus leaving the word *met*, which means "dead." At that moment, the golem is supposed to immediately collapse like a log. But please be cautious as you do so, or you will end up like the Polish rabbi who was crushed under the lifeless mass of his leviathan-like golem.)[8]

An image, however, can take us only so far. What Hobbes's frontispiece cannot *show* is that which can only be *said*. But how can we be sure that what is said will actually be done? This, Agamben explains in the next part of *Homo Sacer*, titled *The Sacrament of Language*, is the very question that sets the political, but also theological, machine in motion. Notwithstanding Hobbes's belief that the force of words is too weak to be binding, he still decided to affix a caption at the top of his frontispiece, as if it were not self-explanatory. The incomplete sentence, borrowed from Job 41:33, is meant to conflate theology and politics, divine and earthly sovereignty, within a single image: "No power on earth is his equal, a creature without fear." (Curiously, the part of the passage after the comma is absent from the engraving, probably because Hobbes knew that, unlike God, the sovereign of flesh and blood is often fearful, exactly like any other human being.) Much more significant, however, is Hobbes's inability to relinquish the palpably paradoxical and unrealistic requirement that every member of the commonwealth willingly pronounce a sort of oath that begins with these words: "I authorize and give up my right of governing myself to this man," the sovereign, who from that point on becomes the sole protector of peace and instigator of war.[9] Agamben shows how the oath (along with its clandestine ally, the curse) stands at the shared origin of both religion and politics, of both divine and earthly law, thus propagating their relentless attempt to control, command, and consecrate living beings. If the oath binds together words and deeds, linguistic beings and living beings, then the curse (which accompanies every oath in case of perjury) signifies the dissolution of this bond. Language is therefore not merely a tool that affirms the glory of God and the sovereign; it does not only reiterate the force of theology and politics. Language is precisely what propels these institutions into being, perpetuates their existence, and maintains their might to this day, which Agamben describes as a stale "governance of empty speech over bare life" (*SL*, 72).

After more than three centuries, the script of *Leviathan* continues to dictate too many plot lines on the stage of world history. Agamben sees the Third Reich as the pinnacle of this baroque tragic drama. In Germany of the early 1930s exceptional measures suspended laws, revoked citizenships, and bypassed basic rights. Certain people, mainly Jews, who were until then an integral part of the state, entered the biopolitical machine that transformed them in less than a decade into the hopeless creatures that occupied the death camps, those bare lives that were stripped of their human form of life, those living beings that no longer deserved to live. In *Remnants of Auschwitz*, the penultimate volume of *Homo Sacer*, Agamben focuses on the most extreme embodiment of this horror: the inhabitants of Auschwitz who were called in the jargon of the camp, for a reason that is still not entirely clear, the *Muselmänner* ("Muslims" in German). Those were the drowned, the inmates who touched bottom, who experienced the limit of human life. But because they had completely lost their ability to use language, they were also unable to bear witness to their inhuman condition. Their existence defied representation. In a rather twisted turn of fate, one can detect today a not entirely different process gradually transforming parts of the world's Muslim population into sacred men and women, like their powerless Semitic brothers and sisters less than a century ago.[10] Although we tend to resist any comparison between the extreme zone of the death camp and the comfort zone in which we live, Auschwitz continues to constitute a sort of negative mirror of the Garden of Eden—into which humanity is repeatedly herded, rather than irrevocably expelled—as new configurations of the biopolitical machine manage to manufacture today results that may seem more elusive but are no less dangerous.

The Biopolitical Ladder

The *Homo Sacer* project, to which Agamben has been dedicating two decades of his life (while we have just tried to condense it into a scant miniature), is rightly considered to be the explosive element in his entire body of work. Although most commentators tend to dwell on, elaborate, and occasionally criticize the biopolitical story put forth in this series of books, we see it only as our impetus rather than as our sole concern. If it is true, as Agamben seems to contend, that the physiology of the political body of the West hides a dangerous pathology, then we can also liken his method of exposing the biopolitical situation to the way in which a scientist isolates the symptoms and causes of a new illness. The symptomatology and etiology of biopolitics may vary. For example, the analysis of capitalism is prominent in competing accounts but is downplayed in Agamben's own research.[11] One should be wary, however, of stretching the medical metaphor beyond its limits by simply reducing biopolitics to some kind of problem with the immune system of the body politic.[12] No matter how one chooses to define the biopolitical syndrome, it is also important not to fall into hypochondria. Just as political action should not be based on the fear of death, the driving force behind political theory should not be any sort of "state-phobia," as Foucault calls it (to which one may add more particular excessive fears, like "sovereignty-phobia," "government-phobia," and "law-phobia").[13] Even more important, we should not forget that symptomatology and etiology are only the first two steps (usually the easier ones) on the way to the much-needed cure. Losing sight of the therapeutic third step that never fails to crop up in Agamben's work is probably the most common way of misconceiving his thought.

A healthier way to approach Agamben's biopolitical studies is to treat them according to Foucault's earliest methodological principle, which stipulates that "original forms of thought are their own introduction: their history is the only kind of exegesis that they permit, and their destiny, the only kind of critique."[14] At this early stage, the scholarly work that tries to comprehend Agamben's intricate thought must first zoom out from the biopolitical story in order to encompass not only decisive elements from his four decades of diverse writings but also his work's delicate and indispensable web of external references. It is misleading, though, to say that *Homo Sacer* really tells us a "story." It is, more accurately, a parable, and as Kafka knew all too well, "if you only followed the parables, you yourselves would become parables."[15] Auschwitz was conceived by the inmates of the camp as the final station at the end of the train line, a point of arrival but never of departure. "We can only say," Agamben writes in a different context, "that here something ends forever and something begins, and that what begins, begins only in what ends" (*IP*, 101). This statement can stand as a succinct epigraph for the *Homo Sacer* project as a whole. Borrowing a Wittgensteinian metaphor, we may therefore go so far as to say that in order to understand Agamben, we must realize that his propositions in *Homo Sacer* are similar to the rungs of a ladder: we need to climb up on these propositions and beyond them, and then *we need to throw the biopolitical ladder away*. Only then we will be able to begin to see the Agambenian world aright.

The Work of Dance in the Age of Sacred Lives

Before we put behind us the biopolitical quandary in order to outline a new political trajectory—or as Agamben likes to call it, the coming politics—it will be helpful to make a short detour and linger on a very curious manifestation of biopolitics, which will take us through a brief history of, believe it or not, ballet. (Disclosure: What follows is not an essential part of this chapter's overall argument, so in case you are in a rush, feel free to skip to the next section.)

Christina, queen of Sweden, was about to celebrate her twenty-third birthday when René Descartes, the fifty-three-year-old "father of modern philosophy," joined her court in Stockholm. Befitting her young age and stature as one of the most powerful persons in Europe at the time, she insisted that Descartes dance in her upcoming court ballet. When the philosopher boldly refused, she demanded instead that he write the libretto for the performance. These are the circumstances that ostensibly led to the composition of Descartes's last text, *The Birth of Peace*, a rather strange addendum to his oeuvre, constituting his only known venture into poetry and politics. Although the authorship of this text has been recently contested, it is difficult not to be struck by the libretto as such.[16] In essence, it is nothing less than a condensed reenactment of Hobbes's *Leviathan* in dance and verse.

The ballet begins with a war of all against all, which subsides only after the middle of the dance, as Pallas—played by Queen Christina herself—enters the stage. Other gods who play secondary roles in the cast possess certain well-known dispositions. For example, Mars loves war while Earth loathes it. If these gods acted in opposition to their inclinations—if Mars suddenly sought peace while Earth rejected it—they would rightfully incur the blame for abandoning their destinies. Pallas (or Christina), on the other hand, is said to lack such a consistent (or constrictive) nature. She is one and the same in both peace and war; thus, it is forbidden to even dare to check or control her judgment. Another striking juxtaposition involves the corps de ballet that plays the cavalrymen. The libretto presents them as supple and strong arms under the command of Pallas, who is presented in turn as their single, shared soul. Here, however, lies what is probably the most subversive element of this dance: the corps de ballet represents the army (and, by synecdoche, the entire populace) as a mere body (*corps*) with no mind of its own; but Pallas, the sovereign, is neither the choreographer nor the librettist nor the spectator but another dancer, a physically present body, rather than a truly ephemeral soul. Pallas is Christina in the flesh, jumping and twirling for the enjoyment of all. Not coincidentally, this idea is encapsulated in her very name: Pallas is another appellation for Athena, the patron deity of the great Greek polis. Whereas Athena's name derives, as Plato explains, from "understanding" and "thought," Pallas's name "derives from her dancing in arms and armor."[17] Whether the story about Descartes's refusal to participate in the dance is true or false, and whether or not he was indeed the author of the libretto of this inflammatory baroque performance, the facts of the matter are that two months after the show the philosopher was found dead, and four years after his death the queen willfully abdicated her throne, spending the rest of her life in exile from Sweden.

The idea that one can speak about dance, that the movement of the dancing body can be articulated and captured in critical and systematic language, that it can be "problematized" (to use Foucault's term), finds its decisive foothold in the Italian peninsula during the fifteenth century. Before this time, the lexicons show little evidence of words that describe specific dance moves. During the Renaissance, however, at least three treatises were dedicated to this subject: the first by Domenico da Piacenza, and two others by his students, Guglielmo Ebreo and Antonio Cornazano. The humanists believed that an eloquent mind was incomplete without an eloquent body. Graceful movement was perceived as a direct manifestation of sharp intelligence. As a consequence, they did not see the dancing body as separated from thought but as much part and parcel of it as language. Dance was conceived for the first time as an art, as an important element in the great art of living. Along with painting, architecture, poetry, and science, dance became an integral part of the edification of human beings. But as the ethos of the Renaissance traveled with Catherine de' Medici across the Alps in the sixteenth century, it was essentially lost in translation. When official foreign dignitaries came to Versailles, the lack of common language was compensated for by the lavish dances orchestrated by Catherine, now the wife of Henry II. Those ballets are some of the earliest examples of statist propaganda, aiming at the glorification of the power of France. They demonstrate how the modern nation-state and "classical" ballet entered the European stage at the same time. Though people always danced and will always dance, the history of ballet is inseparable from the history of modern politics.

So the ideal of the "art of living," which informed the Renaissance discourse on dance, gradually gave way to a discourse about techniques for disciplining bodies and governing them onstage: eloquence transformed into control, and the thinking agent morphed into an obedient apparatus. Even today, the training of the classical ballerina is one of the best examples of the ways that power and knowledge can be inscribed into a human body. Walking, probably the most basic gesture of *Homo sapiens*, is violently altered in two ways: first, the legs turn out rather than forward; and second, the balance between the heel and the toes is rejected in favor of the predominance of the pointe. The ballet schools of the eighteenth and nineteenth centuries even used special mechanical contraptions to achieve these contortions of the dancers' feet. As late as the early twentieth century, a prominent French critic could therefore write: "You may ask whether I am suggesting that the dancer is a machine? But most certainly! It is a machine for manufacturing beauty, if it is in any way possible to conceive of a machine that in itself is a living, breathing thing."[18] But even more than the mechanistic metaphor, ballet dancers were always conceived as the secret symbol of the body politic. The purity and innocence of the ballerina, as she is gracefully lifted by her male companion, signal that her fragile body is offered as the ultimate sacrifice to the sovereign eye of the smug spectator. If there is one figure who embodies in his work these disturbing undercurrents within the field of dance (as Leni Riefenstahl did in cinema, Carl Schmitt in law, and Heidegger in philosophy), it would be Rudolf von Laban. Laban made his name as the inventor of the most influential system of dance notation and as a significant contributor to the transformation of classical ballet into a codified modern practice. It is less known that he also directed, as a dedicated Nazi official under Goebbels, a program that aimed to establish a discipline that he called "total dance." *A Life for Dance*, the title of his 1935 autobiography, conveys in a rather chilling manner the sacrificial myth that the dance community is still struggling to overcome.[19]

The definitive attempt to purge this sacrificial myth—thus marking the true threshold between "classical" ballet and "modern" dance—was undertaken by the Ballet Russes. Despite its name, this company was based in Paris, having left behind it the state-operated ballet schools of Moscow and Saint Petersburg, and distanced itself from institutional political power. Its star dancer, Vaslav Nijinsky, began his career at the age of ten when he entered the Russian Imperial School of Dance. Like the other children there, he was separated from his biological parents and was for all intents and purposes adopted by the tsar. The groundbreaking productions of the Ballet Russes were the ones choreographed by Nijinsky himself. Among his four creations, it was the third, *The Rite of Spring*, that serves as our paradigm. Even though a complete documentation of the original choreography no longer exists, we can safely say the following: Instead of using the classical turnout rotation of the legs, Nijinsky's dancers were asked to awkwardly invert their toes to face each other. Instead of standing on their tiptoes in a futile attempt to touch the sky, they stomped their feet to the ground. The dance tells the story of a human sacrifice during the celebration of spring, an offering for a new beginning. Despite all expectations, Nijinsky did not claim for himself the role of the principal dancer, the one who dances unto death, since he apparently wanted to maintain the traditionally charged symbol of the female ballerina, that perfect sacrificial offering. The uproar that broke out during the premiere in 1913 is by now the stuff of legend. Those who claim that modernity was born at this precise moment (thanks in no small degree to Stravinsky's score) are not necessarily overstating the case.

Five years later, when he was twenty-eight, Nijinsky stopped dancing and choreographing. He began his last recital, which he declared to be about the horrors of the First World War, by telling his audience, "I will show you how we live, how we suffer, how we artists create." He then sat on a chair onstage for half an hour without moving. When he was encouraged by the spectators to begin his dance, he retorted angrily: "How dare you disturb me! I am not a machine. I will dance when I feel like it."[20] At that time, he had already been diagnosed with schizophrenia, from which he suffered for the remaining thirty years of his life. He was treated by the existential psychologist Ludwig Binswanger, to whom he once reported that his body was not his, that someone else moved his body. Whenever anyone tried to approach him during his last years, in which he was essentially an invalid, he still managed to say, very clearly and coherently, "Ne me touchez pas" (Do not touch me), the same words used by the resurrected Christ when approached by Mary Magdalene.[21] "I am the untouchable," perhaps Nijinsky was trying to say, "because my dancing body, which was sacrificed so that others could live, is no longer merely a physical body, just as the glorious body of the dancer onstage is no longer a bare life but a life that cannot be separated from its form." Years after he stopped performing, Nijinsky was asked to dance by an old acquaintance during a visit to his sanatorium. After a long moment of silence and stillness, and to the surprise of all, he suddenly rose on his feet, jumped into the air, and hovered there with his arms and palms stretched to the sides long enough for a photographer to snap a picture. Looking at this image, we are tempted to see in this arrested movement the icon of a new messiah who has done away with the cross, or that of a new sovereign who has done away with both the sword and the staff.[22]

Stéphane Mallarmé asserts that dance is a form of writing, that the body of a dancer writes a poem without writing apparatuses. Hence the notion of choreo-graphy, or dance-writing. Agamben begins "The Body to Come," a short essay about dance (one of his lesser-known interests), by countering this widespread conception: "Dance is not presented here as a writing, but as a reading. Nonetheless, the text to be read is missing; or rather, it is illegible.

According to Hofmannsthal's beautiful image, the dancer 'reads what was never written.'"[23] Modern dance, which has been thriving for the past century since Nijinsky's rise to fame, is a living testament to the possibility of reading what was never written in the book of our modern life. The strong link between ballet and politics just sketched is meant to show why anyone wishing to participate in one of the most promising and urgent intellectual projects of our day, the effort to imagine the politics to come, might well look to modern dance as a pivotal inspiration. As for the skeptics, Baruch Spinoza admonishes, "They still do not know what the body can do."[24]

Ethics After Auschwitz

Even though what can be called the "step-backward-beyond" the biopolitical situation in which we live sounds like a veritable dance move, I will now explore how this can be executed in more conventional philosophical terms.[25] In *Remnants of Auschwitz* Agamben explains why the death camp, which he considers a limit condition, or an extreme situation, is not external to the normal circumstances in which we live but inseparable from them. As often happens in his philosophy, understanding a regular state entails examining the situation once it is pushed to its limits: "The extreme situation's lesson is rather that of absolute immanence, of 'everything being in everything.' In this sense, philosophy can be defined as the world seen from an extreme situation that has become the rule (according to some philosophers, the name of this extreme situation is 'God')" (*RA*, 50). Even though Anaxagoras was the first to suggest that everything is in everything, and Amalric of Bena was the first to apply this formulation to God, the allusion here is first and foremost to Spinoza, and by extension to Deleuze, who emphasized the centrality of the concept of immanence in Spinoza's thought. It is important to note that Agamben's infrequent mention of Spinoza in his texts has no correlation to the actual influence of the *Ethics* on his thought. Spinoza's book is in fact a crucial source for Agamben's own ideas about what he calls the "coming philosophy," since it is a rare example of a successful attempt to resist appealing to a transcendent realm, where one can find either the master of the universe or some unspeakable and unnamable foundation of our existence (*PC*, 238). *Language and Death*, perhaps the definitive work of Agamben's early thought, presents the history of Western metaphysics as an incessant but essentially hopeless search for such an ungrounded ground on which we are supposed to walk, or a silent voice to which we are supposed to listen. The bedrock of our society, he claims, is always revealed at the end to be a void, a self-annihilating nothing. According to his analysis, the ultimate name for the place of negativity at the vanishing core of our culture is "death." Nevertheless, within Spinoza's absolute immanence, where there is nothing outside the single substance that he calls either God or nature, this entire metaphysical castle is revealed to be a house of cards. "In his whole way of living and thinking," Deleuze observes, "Spinoza projects an image of the positive, affirmative life, which stands in contrast with the semblances that men are content with. . . . In a world consumed by the negative, he has enough confidence in life, in the power of life, to challenge death . . . enough confidence in life to denounce all the phantoms of the negative."[26]

As long as the spell of immanence is not cast on the metaphysical machine, it will continue to divide our existence by isolating in it a fictitious ground, by separating from the whole an inaccessible *sacred* realm, an exception to the rule, which is then meant to function as the negative foundation of our existence. In Hegel and Heidegger, "death" indeed takes the position of this ungrounded ground. Nietzsche often derides this nothingness, this negation of life, by calling it "God." Agamben sees his philosophy as an attempt "to absolve man of his ungroundedness and of the unspeakability of the sacrificial mystery" (*LD*, 106). The idea of immanence, this "vertigo of philosophy," as Deleuze calls it, is meant to bring about this desired absolution by calling all separations into question, by rendering the search for a ground redundant (*PC*, 226). If everything is in everything, then the idea that something is fundamentally distinguished from everything else is at best an artificial superfluousness and at worst a nonsensical quibble. For Agamben, the most problematic separation that plagues the history of Western thought is the bifurcation of the concept of life. For example, in Hobbes there is a free-yet-precarious natural life of man-as-wolf on the one hand, and a protected-yet-obedient political life of man-as-citizen on the other. But the list of life divisions is much more pervasive: think about the distinction between nutritive life and sentient life, animal life and human life, biological life and contemplative life, speechless life and linguistic life, and so on. Agamben traces the root of the problem back to the Greek distinction between *zoē* (the fact of being alive) and *bios* (the way of life). Though he acknowledges that, in our culture, the notion of life "cannot be defined," he also observes that "precisely for this reason, [life] must be ceaselessly articulated and divided" through this long list of caesuras and oppositions (*O*, 13). Nevertheless, by following Deleuze, who follows Spinoza, Agamben tries to jam this metaphysical division-machine. By treating life as absolute immanence (and immanence as a life), he brings all those traditional binary oppositions into the zone of indistinction that is the turf on which his philosophy thrives.

Agamben's reading of Deleuze's reading of Spinoza can be misleading in its emphasis on the subject of immanence. In a letter to the English translator of *Expressionism in Philosophy*, Deleuze acknowledges two crucial Spinozistic themes that deeply influenced his thought. The second one is indeed the theme of immanence, on which he felt the need to elaborate in the final years of his life. But the first theme is as much, if not more, fundamentally Deleuzian: "What interested me most in Spinoza," he writes, "wasn't his Substance, but the composition of finite modes."[27] He expands this idea in the third and last part of his major book on Spinoza, though it is present across his entire philosophical work, to the extent that, in the letter, it is almost taken for granted. The idea of a single, infinite, and immanent substance, which can be called either "God" or "nature," as momentous as it is, simply extends a common medieval notion to its logical conclusion. As Harry Wolfson demonstrates, Spinoza's truly radical move was not his definition of substance but that of mode, a concept that up to his time designated the accidents or qualities of different substances.[28] Since there is only one substance, the whole universe is conceived by Spinoza as "affections," as a multiplicity of modes that interact with one another, exist in one another, and are conceived through one another. That modes can simply be understood as "ways" does not mean that they are unnecessary manifestations of actual things. The actual thing does not hide behind its appearance. There is absolutely nothing contingent or fictive about those modes. A particular thing is just a thing in a particular way. As a result (to use Deleuze's favorite example), a workhorse may be more similar to an ox than to a racehorse. If a thing changes its ways, it is no longer the same thing. When a person—this complex constellation of modes—is radically transformed, he is conceived by Spinoza as a different person. "I have no reason to hold," he can therefore conclude, "that a body does not die unless it turns into a corpse."[29] For example, renouncing his Jewish faith was for Spinoza a form of death, or rebirth.

A life is a way. Or better, life is the power to be in some way and *hold on* to this way. If, however, a certain way of being weakens one's existence, then life becomes the power to change one's way and act according to one's own nature. But life is inseparable from its form. Given the numerous apparatuses of the powers that be that try to mold one's mode, or simply disintegrate it (a list that should begin with sovereign power but must extend far beyond), "to live" is "to withstand" or even "to survive" these powers, which can make from one's (form of) life a power in its own right. So instead of gaining *power over life*, which is the ultimate goal of *Leviathan*, Spinoza's book aims to articulate the *power of life* itself, which can be seen as an *inverted biopolitics*. His *Ethics* offers a very effective strategy to resist external powers and to strengthen one's own. But what is truly interesting about this philosophy is that it does not ask people to seek security by severing themselves from the state of nature, by establishing what Spinoza derides as "a kingdom within a kingdom."[30] For his ability to see human life *sub specie naturae*, he is indeed indebted to Hobbes. But his notion of immanence, combined with the concept of mode, enables him to understand Hobbes better than Hobbes understood himself. For Spinoza, our happiness or well-being might be possible even *without* a contract and a sovereign, or even *despite* their existence. As Agamben puts it, "Ethics is the sphere that recognizes neither guilt nor responsibility; it is, as Spinoza knew, the doctrine of the happy life. To assume guilt and responsibility— which can, at times, be necessary—is to leave the territory of ethics and enter that of law. Whoever has made this difficult step cannot presume to return through the door he just closed behind him" (*RA*, 24).

This position should not be confused with another tradition in political philosophy, seemingly opposite to Hobbes's, which does not deride but actually exalts the state of nature, as in Rousseau's *Discourse on Inequality*. One of the inheritors of this attitude is Elsa Morante, whose stories and poems repeatedly articulate this stark distinction between the beatitude of animals and the unhappiness of the multitude of humans (children, along with select adults—she specifically mentions Spinoza as being one of them—are sometimes treated in her writings as a sort of a threshold between the two groups). Agamben explains: "The wound that traverses Elsa's work is not simply, as in Spinoza, the divergence between forms of life, the discordant plurality of the different modes of expressing a single substance. It is instead a fracture that passes through the inside of life itself, dividing it like the sharpest blade according to whether or not it remained in Eden and whether or not it was contaminated by the shadow of knowledge" (*EP*, 106). Agamben does not share this nostalgic fiction of an animalistic, pure innocence, which he eventually came to understand as a sacred life that can easily be harmed. What looks like blessedness turns out to bear much more misery than one may assume, since those who are "saved" from our fallen civilization can also be seen as forsaken by it. Here it is important to mention the Heideggerian critique of Rilke's suggestion that humans are forever trapped by their own devices, while animals live in what the poet calls "the open" (*O*, 57–62). Nevertheless, Agamben's philosophy does not really take part in, but rather decisively breaks from, this contentious debate between Heidegger, Hobbes, Morante, Rilke, Rousseau, and so many others about how to draw the line between man and animal, culture and nature. Like Spinoza, he no longer strives to separate one from the other in a definitive, essential, or metaphysical way. Instead of claiming that man must master nature or that nature must master man, he tries to localize a zone of indifference between the speaking being and the living being, where the only mastery is of the relationship or "the play between the two terms" (*O*, 83). Rather than try to articulate the abyss between the human and the inhuman, he insists that "human beings are human insofar as they bear witness to the inhuman" (*RA*, 121). This move allows us to begin to see a multiplicity of modes, of forms of life, instead of being mired in life's simplistic and exhausted dualisms.

The Potentiality of Thought

If Hobbes is the father of modern politics as we know it from the daily headlines, then the "blessed thorn" (the meaning of "Baruch" in Hebrew and "Spinoza" in Portuguese) is the father of a sort of underground political movement, or an alternative practical philosophy.[31] Despite the canonization of the *Ethics* by academic philosophy, it still struggles to express its radical way of thinking and living. If Spinoza's age—and his life—were marked by the fight against the religious establishment, then our times—and our lives—are marked by a not dissimilar attempt to grapple with the political one. His excommunication from his Jewish congregation is duplicated today to the nth degree in the ban or expulsion of millions of individuals from countries around the world as refugees or personae non gratae, which deems a great part of the world's population politically and economically irrelevant. It is thus not a surprise that his ideas lose none of their relevance when they are translated from the theological to the political, from the seventeenth to the twenty-first century. Spinoza can therefore serve as the force behind the transformation of Hobbes's modern politics of bare life into Agamben's coming politics of form of life.

When considered in opposition to Hobbes's, Spinoza's political philosophy is usually presented as a variation on the liberal-democratic theme. This line of analysis is of little help from Agamben's perspective, where the usual political dichotomies are virtually expendable. Nevertheless, it is instructive to see how in 1938 Carl Schmitt could still marvel at how "a small intellectual switch emanating from the nature of Jewish life accomplished, with the most simple logic and in the span of a few years, the decisive turn in the fate of the leviathan." According to Schmitt, Spinoza revealed "the barely visible crack" in Hobbes's justification for the sovereign state in such a way that "the leviathan's vitality was sapped from within and life began to drain out of him."[32] He did so by deeming thought (along with perception and expression) as paramount, while treating the state organization as a mere condition meant only to facilitate thinking. The state, however, is not a *necessary* condition, without which it would be impossible to think. But without thinking any state would surely crumble and die. The "liberal Jew," as Schmitt used to refer to Spinoza, might therefore deserve this label only as long as it points to the single freedom and the single practice that was truly dear to his heart, which is the Archimedean point of his entire political theology: the *libertas philosophandi*, the freedom to philosophize. The exceptional zone where one can never be constrained by the political and theological powers is called, after all, *thinking*. But this is not to say that one is reduced, as in Descartes, to the futility of an inner and solitary thinking-thing. As the fourth part of the *Ethics* demonstrates, the book is not really about an individualistic quest for knowledge but about a way of thinking, and hence of living, that is essentially a shared enterprise. What brings us together is not a common place, birth, law, or leader but our common endeavor *to understand*. The ability of people to partake in the same experience of thought, to share the same receptivity or sensibility, to follow the same reason, is what enables them to live in Spinoza's coming community. Thinking, reasoning, and understanding are not merely epistemological faculties but ethico-political ones. Even if in Spinoza a thought cannot affect a body and a body cannot affect a thought, a thought can certainly engender other thoughts, which necessarily (even if unnoticeably) manifest themselves in the material world, and not only in the realm of ideas. Perhaps this is what stands behind Bertolt Brecht's claim that politics is nothing other than "the art of thinking inside other people's heads."[33]

Of course, it would be ironic to suggest that Spinoza was the sole progenitor of the idea of a collective intellectual undertaking. Agamben traces this potent belief back to Averroes, who promoted in the twelfth century the notion of "possible intellect." Humans are "cohabitants," as it were, within the possible intellect, in which their own singular and limited perspective participates. But the possible intellect, Averroes maintains, remains unique, eternal, and unaffected by the particular ideas entertained in the minds of mortal individuals. What still enables the mediation or connection between individual intellects and the possible intellect (and thus prevents the latter from becoming an unapproachable transcendent entity) is what medieval psychology called "phantasms," or images that are closely linked with the faculty of imagination (S, 83). By invoking this abstruse theory, Agamben goes so far as to claim that "modern political philosophy does not begin with classical thought, which had made of contemplation, of the *bios theoreticos*, a separate and solitary activity ('exile of the alone to the alone') but rather only with Averroism, that is, with the thought of the one and only possible intellect common to all human beings" (*ME*, 10).

Despite Agamben's seemingly fragmentary style, it is possible to locate here a persistent theme of his writings. "Thought" is one of his central notions, and it carries not only theoretical implications but also personal ones. He has (something that cannot be called anything other than) faith that the power of study can open the path to thought, that intellectual work has the capacity to contribute to thought, or Thought. (This attitude, however, should not be confused with what is called in academia, with too much institutional bad faith and too little personal integrity, "contribution to the discourse.") The best catchphrase to describe this position would be the one Agamben chose for the Italian edition of his major essay collection: "The Potentiality of Thought."[34] A definitive formulation of this position can be found in his manifesto, "Form-of-Life," where he writes: "I call *thought* the nexus that constitutes forms of life in an inseparable context as form-of-life. . . . To think does not mean merely to be affected by this or that thing, by this or that content of an enacted thought, but rather at once to be affected by one's own receptiveness and experience in each and every thing that is thought, by a pure potentiality of thinking."[35] Agamben is not satisfied with the relativistic claim that there is a plurality of ways of living, just as it was not enough for Spinoza to posit the divergence of multiple modes expressing a single God. They are both convinced that without some communicative nexus that connects the elements, their separation will lead to impotence and hence to bondage. Agamben's and Spinoza's supreme aim is not really to find a way to connect the individual's thought to God's, or God to nature, but to link us to one another through our shared capacity to think (though without the necessity of a universal rationality), through our ability to be receptive to a shared experience (without the need to have the same perspective), and even by our tendency to come to some understanding about our shared situation (which is always incomplete and fragmentary). When we do so, we become powerful; when we don't, there is no "we." If for Hobbes sovereign power brings together a multitude of human bodies in order to establish a state, for Agamben the potentiality of thought is the unitary power by which our different forms of life come together as "form-of-life." Form-of-life is what calls for thinking; the task of thinking is to imagine this form-of-life. Here we encounter the guiding concept of Agamben's entire political philosophy. (In order not to give the impression that Agamben's way of understanding "form-of-life" is identical to the way this notion is developed in the present book, we will not use his hyphenated phrase and will make do with "form of life." In this context it may be said that form-of-life is to form of life what potentiality is to actuality.)

It is crucial to note, however, that for Agamben "political philosophy" is a redundant expression, just like "plant botany." "For politics," he writes, "has no name other than its Greek pseudonym, which is barely uttered here: philosophy" (PC, 85). Ultimately, the goal of philosophy and politics is the same: "the full enjoyment of worldly life" (ME, 114). This is not necessarily to say that philosophers should address particular political issues, nor does it mean that they should advise politicians or, heaven forbid, become politicians themselves. Having no aspiration to obtain sovereign power or to visibly clash with this defunct power, the philosopher may even give the sovereign what belongs to the sovereign. Categorically, philosophy must never serve any established power. Whereas the spectacular politics that we are well familiar with is best summed up in John Adams's *spectemur agendo* (let us be seen in action), the politics that Agamben has in mind returns to the Epicurean *lathe biosas* (live in hiding), which Arendt calls "the *topos*, the locality, of the man who thinks."[36] But in Agamben there is a complete reversal of Epicurus's retreat from the political sphere. Some ancient thinkers found refuge from the dangers of life by withdrawing into thought, but our modern situation is quite the opposite: the thinker typically lives a rather safe and routine life. The true danger, then, lies in the thought itself.[37] This is not to say, to follow Arendt once again, that there are "dangerous thinkers" or "dangerous thoughts" but that from the perspective of the unthinking masses and those who control them, only "thinking itself is dangerous," since the very act of thought is a priori an affront.[38] For Agamben, the usual philosophical gesture of retreat is therefore never away from politics but always toward it.

As hinted previously, if Agamben had the opportunity to personally thank one individual for inspiring his unique position at the threshold between politics and philosophy (and the best way to thank, as Heidegger used to say, is to think), it would probably be Hannah Arendt. More particularly, he owes thanks to *Thinking*, the first book in her posthumously published *The Life of the Mind*. "Practically," she writes there, "thinking means that each time you are confronted with some difficulty in life you have to make up your mind anew."[39] Ethically, one can add, it means that the true axis of evil—first and foremost in the smallest, most everyday matters—is more often than not simply called thoughtlessness (and not, as Plato maintains, ignorance). This, of course, is not to say that thinkers are protected from participating in evil (like Heidegger and Schmitt) or suffering from evil (like Benjamin and Jean Améry). When politics is reduced to biopolitics, *anyone* can occupy, even for a short period of time, the position of the victimizing sovereign or the victimized *homo sacer* (in both cases, thinking simply becomes superfluous). Besides, thought is not at all the exclusive possession of thinkers, especially not of those whom Arendt teasingly calls "professional thinkers." Thinking can be found, or not, virtually everywhere: it traverses, and thus puts into question, not only basic separations such as those between theory and practice, speech and action, spirituality and corporeality, understanding the world and changing it, but also more mundane divisions such as master and slave, high and low culture, work and home, public and private. A hand gesture or a dress pleat can be as intelligent as a book or a plan. And wherever a thought manifests itself, there politics is being reborn. This is precisely the reason why

Agamben treats "thought" and "politics" as synonymous (*IP*, 98). But if Aristotle's claim that "the actuality [rather than the potentiality] of thought is life" is taken as seriously as it should be, then "thinking" and "living" also become two notions that must constantly feed and explain and expose one another.[40] One may then begin to see oneself, one's own life, as something thought.[41]

The Color of Potentiality

It is not so easy to represent the very act of thinking. Cinema, for example, has great difficulty fulfilling this goal. We hear many complaints about the way various social types are depicted in film, but we rarely notice that it is actually "the thinker" who is misrepresented in the most grotesque manner: either as an idler or a rascal, who tends to be charismatic, awkward, eccentric, or simply deranged. In order to invoke the actual act of thinking, filmmakers revert to those embarrassing "Eureka!" scenes, or to those montages of the thinker shuffling papers while some entrancing string music plays in the background. Needless to say, this has little to do with our personal experience of thinking. Even when every possible distraction is stripped from the scene, and all that is left is a single person in front of a rolling camera (as in Warhol's so-called screen tests), more often than not the traces of thought are covered up by an overwhelming sense of boredom.

Still photography, by contrast, seems almost to have been invented for the sake of capturing thought. For example, if a good photographer manages to catch an appealing thinker when he or she is not pretentiously gazing into the horizon, or pressing a finger into his or her left temple, then the picture is usually as mesmerizing as a picture can be. Even glossy fashion photography cannot erase the thought from the model's face. Even in our personal photo album there are probably more signs of thought in the most casual snapshot of a loved one (even of a baby) than in almost any scene from the history of cinema. Thinking, which tends to be lost on the silver screen, is redeemed in the millisecond of the camera shutter's opening and closing.

Every activity moves the rusty wheels of history slightly forward, whereas thinking is the special act that *arrests* this movement. Photography and thought thus have a secret affinity: they both somehow manage (quite miraculously, it must be admitted) to stop time. Maybe they can do so because they function a little like the comma in a sentence: "Where the voice drops," Agamben writes, "where breath is lacking, a little sign remains suspended. On nothing other than that, hesitantly, thought ventures forth" (*IP*, 104). Thinking is therefore very different from regular work, because it is a resolutely "inactive" act or an "inoperative" operation, which suspends rather than perpetuates the progress of world history. Agamben intentionally avoids talking about the actualization of thought not because he is an idealist but because he thinks about thinking as a reality that must be reckoned with as such rather than as the mere cause or germ of some action in the "real world." His conviction is that the potentiality of thought must always remain alive, without ever being exhausted in or depleted by a certain actuality, no matter how awful the situation seems to be or how wonderful it may come to be. For the sake of this argument, potentiality may thus be likened to the film in a camera before it is exposed to light and impressed with a particular situation in the world. When we look at the true image of thought, what we see is not this or that colorful picture of an actual state of affairs but, once again, simply "darkness," which is, according to Agamben, "in some way the color of potentiality" (*PC*, 180).

Feather-Light Rubble

Zarathustra's Whisper

Ever since Plato witnessed his master's last breath, philosophers have been incessantly, and sometimes obsessively, analyzing the notion of death. For some odd reason, they are less comfortable speaking about the question of life, so much so that when Nietzsche (who is usually very straightforward about this question) wanted to articulate the relationship of philosophy to life, he decided to revert to an allegory whose meaning is still shrouded in fog. Let us, then, begin with a short excursus that may help cast Agamben's own philosophy of life in the right light.

There are two "Dancing Songs" in *Thus Spoke Zarathustra*. They are both presented as love songs, depicting the relationship between the protagonist and a woman named Life. This seemingly serene romance gets complicated (and interesting) when it becomes clear that Zarathustra is also involved with another woman, called Wisdom. Despite his devotion to Life, he also has a peculiar attraction to this Wisdom. "For thus matters stand among the three of us," he avows: "Deeply I love only Life—and verily, most of all when I hate Life. But that I am well disposed towards Wisdom, and often too well, that is because she reminds me so much of Life. She has her eyes, her laugh, and even her little golden fishing rod: is it my fault that the two look so similar?"[1] Zarathustra tries to offer here an explanation for his inability to remain loyal to Life. Wisdom's allure, so he claims, is a result of her uncanny *resemblance* to Life. This, I will show, is more than a lame excuse. The issue becomes more evident in the next stanza, when Zarathustra summons the courage to tell Life about the other woman. Instead of being outraged, Life only "laughed sarcastically and closed her eyes," wondering out loud about Wisdom's true identity: "'Of whom are you speaking?' she asked; 'no doubt, of me. And even if you are right—should *that* be said to my face?'"[2] This strange reproach seems to portray Zarathustra as a fool, in opposition to Life, who appears to be in full control of the ticklish situation. We also need to bear in mind that Zarathustra's devotion to Life knows no bounds. In the beginning of the "Other Dancing Song" he confesses: "I fear you near, I love you far; your flight lures me, your seeking cures me: I suffer, but what would I not gladly suffer for you?"[3] But still, Wisdom's seduction is sweet and strong, and Zarathustra's love for Life appears to be gradually fading away. As the second "Dancing Song" proceeds, we hear the pleading words of Life, who is now utterly devastated as her lover plans his final departure. She professes her jealousy toward Wisdom and tells her partner: "If your Wisdom ever runs away from you, then my love would quickly run away from you too."[4] No doubt, there is definitely something very strange about this triangular love affair. Even though Life shows obvious disdain toward Wisdom, her relationship with Zarathustra is absolutely symmetrical to his relationship with Wisdom. The two women look the same, act the same, and love the same. So why would Zarathustra want to leave Life for another woman who is exactly like her? And why does Life claim that she would stop loving Zarathustra the moment Wisdom abandons him? The answer is to be found at the end of Nietzsche's little soap opera. It begins when Zarathustra admits that he is indeed about to leave Life for good:

> Then Life looked back and around thoughtfully and said softly: "O Zarathustra, you are not faithful enough to me. You do not love me nearly as much as you say; I know you are thinking of leaving me soon." . . .
>
> "Yes," I answered hesitantly, "but you also know—" and I whispered something into her ear, right through her tangled yellow foolish tresses.
>
> "You *know* that, O Zarathustra? Nobody knows that."
>
> And we looked at each other and gazed on the green meadow over which the cool evening was running just then, and we wept together. But then Life was dearer to me than all my Wisdom ever was.[5]

Remember that just a moment ago Zarathustra told Life that he was about to abandon her. But right after he whispered the secret that "nobody knows," the couple looked at each other and then gazed at the green meadow below. Whether their tears are of joy and the ending is a happy one is not absolutely clear, though it certainly seems so, as the love of Zarathustra for Life appears to triumph, and the affair he had with Wisdom is somehow forgotten and forgiven.

So what did Zarathustra whisper into the ear of Life? This question is the cipher to Nietzsche's dancing songs, as well as to an underlying conviction that seems to inform Agamben's philosophical thought. About a dozen scholars have tried to solve this mystery in recent years. One group maintains that Zarathustra's secret is the eternal recurrence: that even though he is about to leave Life, eventually he will come back.[6] The second group claims that Zarathustra whispers that he is about to die, so, by leaving Life, he executes his death wish.[7] The sense one gets from surveying the relevant literature dedicated to this episode is, as one scholar concludes, "that life is fundamentally tragic, but that this tragedy is, as Zarathustra says next to life, dearer to him than all his wisdom."[8] There is, however, a completely different way to understand what Zarathustra whispers into Life's ear through her golden tresses. It encapsulates a new way of thinking about this secret that, in opposition to all the available interpretations, attempts to offer "a thought that affirms life and the will to life, a thought which finally expels the whole of the negative," as Deleuze positions Nietzsche's true philosophical legacy.[9] After Life said that she knows that Zarathustra is about to leave her, he whispered into her ear something along these lines: "But you also know that Wisdom is not another woman, but simply you, O Life, in disguise." The two women only appear to be distinguishable. The notions of life and wisdom, which are often portrayed as women throughout Nietzsche's writings, are revealed in the two dancing songs, by means of an abundance of not very complicated clues, to be one and the same.

From this perspective, it appears that it was not Zarathustra who played with Life's heart but Life who fooled Zarathustra all along, disguising herself as another woman, seducing her own man. Zarathustra only imagined that he was a cheater, hiding his secret behind Life's back. In reality, he never left her. But perhaps Zarathustra actually knew about this sham all along, and this was nothing but mischievous role-playing: Life pretended to be Wisdom, and Zarathustra pretended not to know. This, however, is not to suggest that after the secret had been divulged, Zarathustra and Life lived happily ever after, that the intimacy between the two transformed this enigmatic woman called "Life" into an open book, that Life irrevocably moved from concealment to unconcealment. As much as you feel close to life, life will always remain closed to you, because love, Agamben writes, entails an ability "to live in intimacy with a stranger, not in order to draw him closer, or to make him known, but rather to keep him strange, remote: unapparent—so unapparent that his name contains him entirely. And, even in discomfort, to be nothing else, day after day, than the ever open place, the unwaning light in which that one being, that thing, remains forever exposed and sealed off" (*IP*, 61).

"Love," Jean-Luc Nancy adds, "forms the limit of a thinking that carries itself to the limit of philosophy."[10] The most plausible implication of Nietzsche's dancing songs has to do with precisely this "love of wisdom," the meaning of philosophy according to its Greek etymology. This love, Nietzsche seems to claim, explains nothing but is itself in need of explanation. The truth is that there is only one woman that philosophers can love dearly, and the name of this woman is not really Wisdom but Life (pardon the chauvinism). At best, Wisdom is simply Life in disguise. Also, Life is not an obedient woman, waiting for the philosophers to return home from their reckless escapades. She is less like Penelope and more like Nastasya Filippovna. "We love life," Nietzsche admits, "not because we are used to living, but because we are used to loving. There is always some madness in love. But there is always also some reason in madness."[11] In short, the secret that "nobody knows" is actually something that seems, in retrospect, pretty obvious: the philosophical love of wisdom is just a front for the much more profound, though much less manifest, love of life.

Sharpening Knives

Despite the multitude of fairly explicit and quite systematic references to the notion of life scattered throughout Agamben's philosophy, it would be imprudent to restrict ourselves to these references alone. If it is true that the "wisdom" of a philosopher is to be found not in his or her specific comments about the subject matter of wisdom but in the philosophy as such and as a whole, then the same holds true concerning the topic of "life." Taking the comparison one step further, we may even say that in the same manner that philosophers are not wise but only the lovers of wisdom, it is also true that, as much as they love life, they are also rarely fully alive. But when the philosophical work is closely tied to the labor of life, as is the case with Agamben's lifework, an attention to the former cannot fail to illuminate the latter. In other words, if there is a way of life that is made manifest in Agamben's philosophy, one should first look for the way this philosophy is done, even before searching for anything specific that it has to say about the subject matter of life.

Above all, it should be noted that Agamben's thought does not seek definitive metaphysical grounds. Instead, it tries to offer various ethical and political means, which themselves lack a determinate end. Since his philosophical practice is dedicated to the discovery of what he calls "means without end," his work can be described as an attempt to "make means meet" (not their end but each other). His texts do their best to avoid being "a static archetype," as he puts it in a different context, "but rather a constellation in which phenomena are composed in a gesture" (*IH*, 153). There are therefore no necessary essences but only possible ways of thinking and living. True, he usually engages only in theoretical work, but his studies are great examples of the way theory can have palpable implications and a real effect, whereas so many "actions in the real world" that people believe they should undertake can be rather impractical and ineffective. With an unexpected nod to pragmatists from C. S. Peirce to J. L. Austin, Agamben seems to be very attentive to what a text can *do*. Though he avoids the question "*What* shall we do?" since it is a rather empty inquiry that leads to paralysis rather than to action, he is always drawn to frame more focused questions that can lead to concrete and practical answers about *how* to do and think about certain things, *how* to act and be in certain situations, though the possibilities implied in his philosophy are never sealed off from future interpretations or appropriations. This priority of the "how" over the "what" in Agamben's work entails, first of all, that "What is philosophy?" (the question that informs this chapter) henceforth morphs into the less obvious "How is philosophy?" The same fate awaits the guiding question of this book as a whole: "What is Agamben's philosophy of life?" Leaving aside the phrasing of such questions, we find that it is already clear that their answers must be political and ethical to their very core. Here lies what may be Agamben's most enduring legacy: not merely what but how he thinks. The fact that he never bothers to give this "how" a catchy name should not deceive us. Without committing himself to one of the available restrictive "readings" that we impose upon the world (Marxist, postcolonialist, poststructuralist, psychoanalytic, deconstructionist, feminist, and the list goes on, though not for long), and without indoctrinating his readers into a new school of thought, Agamben's oeuvre has the potential to bring about a paradigm shift in the way we do theoretical work.

We normally like to call these considerations "the *method* of the philosopher," but since method comes from *hodos*, Greek for "way," one may also speak of "the way of the philosopher." The problem, however, is that methodological discussions tend to give the impression, as Heidegger once remarked, of people sharpening knives when there is nothing left to cut.[12] We might also assume that *The Signature of All Things*, the work in which Agamben explicitly confronts the question of his own method, would be the only place to search for a firsthand guide to this problematic yet indispensable subject. But as often happens with many of Agamben's writings, which tend to maintain an air of suspense, much is left unsaid in that short book. I will therefore try to thematize a few of his less explored or not fully explicit methodological concerns. The aim of the following vignettes is to make manifest the distinct way of living that emerges from Agamben's unique way of thinking: to reveal the form of life encapsulated in the gestures and signatures embedded in his philosophy. If at times this exercise looks like sectarian knife sharpening, it is only because today there is so much that needs to be cut.

Emergency Brake

The scholars of the future who take it upon themselves to read the stories told by the past few generations will not fail to notice, as we already have noticed, the numerous narratives that take place in or around trains. Though I have no intention of embarking on a survey of the relevant literature dedicated to trains as a primary locus of the modern imagination, it would still be worthwhile to mention two of Foucault's observations: The first is that the train is an extraordinary "other space," as he calls it, since it is "something through which one goes, it is also something by means of which one can go from one point to another, and then it is also something that goes by."[13] His second observation is that people used to think about the railroad as an apparatus that could usher in world peace, since it was hoped that rail travelers, when exposed to other countries and cultures, would no longer breed animosity and misunderstanding. This dream dissipated when, after the Second World War, other uses of the train became apparent.[14]

Instead of moving on from the train to other prominent sites of our more recent imagination (such as the airport or the hotel), I would like to linger on an important twist that can be found in many of those train narratives. I am referring to the moment when the entire train suddenly comes to a halt in the middle of nowhere because there is something, or someone, on the tracks, and the passengers find themselves in unfamiliar surroundings that no longer pass by but stay put; or the moment in which the passengers realize that their car has been disconnected from the rest of the train and is left motionless in the middle of a bridge; or stories about trains that fail to leave the station; or about stations in which an expected train never arrives. In one of Benjamin's notes for his final essay dedicated to the concept of history, the philosophical significance of those somewhat unsettling, somewhat liberating trains at a standstill becomes clear: "Marx says that revolutions are the locomotive of world history. But perhaps it is quite otherwise. Perhaps revolutions are an attempt by the passengers on this train—namely, the human race—to activate the emergency brake."[15] We tend to think that revolutions are an effort to change the world, but we habitually forget the other side of the coin, which asserts that every revolution also tries to establish an enduring world order. Benjamin's sentiment, however, lies on neither side of this dialectical currency. Since a revolution is a brake and not a break, it is precisely this dialectics that he wishes to bring to a standstill (the word he uses is *Stillstellung*, his own neologism, which may bring to mind the stoppage of a machine). As he explains elsewhere, "Every presentation of history [must] begin with awakening; in fact, it should treat of nothing else," which is possibly an echo of James Joyce's "history is a nightmare from which I am trying to awake."[16] Most likely, the nightmare in question involves some kind of train wreck.

It is very difficult to look at anything today other than through the lens of development. Everything in life must evolve or devolve, fold or unfold, progress or decline, for better or for worse. Even a thought is understood as a "train of thought," which is an obvious contradiction, at least in Agamben's mind, since as we have previously seen, the point about thinking is that it can halt the moving train. Although most thinkers have little tolerance for *arrested* development, Agamben's intolerance is directed toward development as such: the train that has lost its brakes while half of humanity is on board, unable to get off, while the other half stands by the tracks, unable to get on. "This is why," Agamben declares in no uncertain terms, "we do not want new works of art or thought; we don't want another epoch of culture and society: what we want is to save the epoch and society from their wandering in tradition, to grasp the *good*—undeferable and non-epochal—which was contained in them. The undertaking of this task would be the only ethics, the only politics which measures up to the moment" (*IP*, 88).

Living at a dialectical standstill allows us to finally put aside this nagging need to always be up to date with whatever goes on, to let go of the Hegelian demand to be a child of one's time. Instead, our role model becomes Rilke's disinherited children, "to whom no longer what's been, and not yet what's coming, belongs."[17] The person who is truly contemporary, Agamben adds in a similar spirit, is not the one who perfectly coincides with the present but the one whose life does not exactly synchronize with his or her times—the one whose relationship with the age is slightly out of sync or out of joint, on the threshold between the "no more" and the "not yet" (*WA*, 40–41). This is where I would like to position Agamben's own thought and the life that aligns with it. Consider in this respect the life that is "not yet" at the moment of birth, and the life that is "no more" that we call death. Even though death positions one's entire life as "what has been," and birth means that one's whole life is "what is coming," the experiences of one's mortality and natality are not restricted to those definite boundaries or limit conditions. Every moment of living and thinking is charged with this bipolar tension. Even if I am presently a being-in-the-world, as Heidegger claims, a part of me is not-yet-living-in-the-world and a part of me is no-longer-living-in-the-world (I am, after all, still a being in time). To use the terms of modal logic, we could say that what informs the life of the person whom Rilke calls "the disinherited" and Agamben calls "the contemporary" is neither the sealed *necessity* and *impossibility* of the one stuck in the past, nor is it even the *contingency* and *possibility* of the one who beholds the future. Instead, this life, while still trying to grasp what has been and gather what is coming, operates in the *exigency* that can arise only from an ability to face the darkness of the present. Kafka hits the nail on the head when he writes about those "travelers in a train that has met with an accident in a tunnel, and this at a place where the light of the beginning can no longer be seen, and the light of the end is so very small a glimmer that the gaze must continually search for it and is always losing it again, and, furthermore, it is not even certain whether it is the beginning or the end of the tunnel."[18]

Strange as it may seem, a thought at a standstill can be effectively suspended between, rather than be burdened by, the glimmers of whence and whither, origin and destiny, damnation and redemption, history and prophecy. The Agambenian way of thinking, as it remains immobile and immediate, operates within the field of tensions generated by these bipolar oppositions. Only a thought that keeps its distance from both sides can charge life with a potential power capable of answering its exigent demands. Like Kafka's Barnabas, the messenger in the white suit who tries to connect between the official Klamm and the protagonist K., Agamben found a way to mediate—by means of his writings—between the cryptic sender in the impenetrable castle of tradition and the clueless addressee who feels, to be honest, somewhat lost in the village below: "Since the goal is already present and thus no path exists that could lead there," he writes, "only the perennially late stubbornness of a messenger whose message is nothing other than the task of transmission can give back to man, who has lost his ability to appropriate his historical space, the concrete space of his action and knowledge" (*MC*, 114).

In Agamben, Zeno's paradoxes of motion (such as the one about the arrow in flight that in every moment is at rest, or the one about the race in which Achilles never catches up to the tortoise) are used as parables with ethical and political implications, meant to positively guide and inform, rather than daze and confuse, the way we not only think but also live.

Above the Weight of the World

Let us reframe our question by considering another analogy, which is quite popular in philosophical circles: that of the building. Philosophers often see themselves as builders or demolishers. The most ambitious ones tend to think that they can do both, whereas the slightly more modest ones try to engage in the necessary side work associated with this ever-evolving and often lucrative real estate enterprise. Life, in this sense, is distinguished from philosophy as tenants are distinguished from the building that is being erected or dismantled with little attention to their needs. The difficulty that people have in accepting Walter Benjamin as a bona fide philosopher has something to do with the fact that this game of de- and con-struction is at a complete stalemate in his work. Rather than offer any specifications for a building's architectonic plan, his work may be described as the building's archeology. It has often been observed that his texts neither dismantle nor assemble anything but wander instead across a land scattered with ruins. By closely attending to the remains of our industrious tradition, to the fragments of our intellectual culture, he is said to be "crystallizing" those obscure and forgotten elements, or to be "redeeming" them from their perpetual exchange in the marketplace of ideas. By finding a new use within his own work for these *disjecta membra*, he seems to breathe into them a new life, or an afterlife. But what is much less apparent, though much more important, about Benjamin's method is that the condition of *survival*—which should be understood here in its etymological sense of outliving, overliving, hyperliving, or posthumous life—pertains to the philosopher himself before it applies to the elements of his philosophy. The remnant that is here at stake is not merely an item that belonged to a bygone historical age and was then salvaged by the "retro" thinker in the present age. Instead, like those solitary characters in science fiction stories who come upon the remains of their own civilization after its apocalyptic extinction, the philosopher, and not just his philosophy, can assume the role of the remnant.

Though Agamben clearly inherits from this Benjaminian dialectics at a standstill, from a purely stylistic point of view (which may also merely be my subjective view) he also departs from his predecessor in at least one intriguing way. Benjamin's texts always seem to twist, curl, convolute, and turn back upon themselves. They are like a labyrinth with many entrances and no discernible exit. Though they are explicitly meant to lead to the reader's awakening, they usually give the impression of a dreamscape rather than an alarm clock (Benjamin's last essay on the concept of history is a decisive exception). In Agamben, on the other hand, the rubble in which the philosopher wanders tends to lose its weight, which usually enables him to shrug off the burden of its heavy past. This allows his prose not exactly to soar but, in a sense, to levitate slightly above the wasteland of tradition. It is not uncommon for writers to get bogged down by the texts that they analyze. Even what Agamben once called "the deconstructionist factory," which promised to destabilize the foundational texts of our culture, more often than not just left us ensnared by them (*EP*, 77). By contrast, Agamben's work proves that to "master a text" means not only that one knows it inside out but, even more decisively, that the interpreter is not enslaved by the text. An echo of this line of thought may be heard in one of Ingeborg Bachmann's posthumously published poems:

The Radical Means
Wasteland, but only to the eye
that serves life,
feather-light rubble.[19]

Is it possible that, in the hands of the radical thinker—for whom life is something that one masters rather than serves—the debris that piles up with the progress of history can become as light as a page in a book? It certainly appears to be the case if we consider another adamant promoter of the value of lightness, who, like Bachmann, was also a friend of Agamben. Italo Calvino died prematurely in 1985 while preparing his Norton Lectures, which were supposed to be delivered later that year at Harvard. From his notes, published after his death as *Six Memos for the Next Millennium*, we know that he intended to devote the opening lecture to the subject of lightness. One of his leading claims there is that (in opposition to what certain writers of popular cultural theory may lead you to believe) lightness need not collapse into frivolity, that it is possible to imagine a "thoughtful lightness," as he calls it. In what reads as either a prophecy or a will, Calvino writes: "Were I to choose an auspicious image for the new millennium, I would choose that one: the sudden agile leap of the poet-philosopher who raises himself above the weight of the world, showing that with all his gravity he has the secret of lightness, and that what many consider to be the vitality of the times—noisy, aggressive, revving and roaring—belongs to the realm of death, like a cemetery for rusty cars."[20] Attempting, perhaps, to distance his position from the one promoted in Milan Kundera's *The Unbearable Lightness of Being*—where nothing is consequential and everything is permitted because life is lighter than air—Calvino repeatedly evokes the heaviness of life and the world in which we live. He therefore presents the kind of literature that adheres to the secret of lightness as a way to keep this world and life aloft. In this way, he invites a rather problematic dichotomy: weightless writing as opposed to weighty living. The question, then, is whether—and if so, how—Agamben's poetic philosophy manages to approach both the written and the lived with a lightness that is not only bearable but also thoughtful.

The Stillest Word

To better understand how Agamben develops Benjamin's dialectics at a standstill, we need to contrast it with the work of Theodor Adorno and his circle (which basically held the monopoly on Benjamin's thought for almost half a century). For us to begin to see the difference between Adorno's "damaged life" that "does not live" and Agamben's own notion of life, the conventional building and train analogies need to give way to a less obvious one: the fairy tale about the frog-prince, this happy inversion of Kafka's *Metamorphosis*. We are all familiar with this tale about the old witch who transforms a handsome prince into a frog, and the young maiden who has to kiss that slimy frog in order to reverse the spell and win the love of her life. (Folklorists are, in fact, unsure about the origin of the prevalently modern kiss element. In older versions, the maiden removes the spell by either slamming the frog against a wall or intimately sharing her bed with it.) In Agamben's stark retelling of this story, the frog-prince is used as an allegory for history, while Benjamin plays the role of the maiden and Adorno that of the witch:

> Dialectical historicism, whose spokesman [Adorno] is, is the witch who, after turning the prince into a frog, believes she holds within the magic wand of dialectics the secret of any possible transformation. But [Benjamin's] historical materialism is the maiden who kisses the frog right on the mouth, and breaks the dialectical spell. For whereas the witch knows that since every prince is really a frog, every frog can become a prince, the maiden does not know this, and her kiss touches precisely what the frog and the prince have in common. (*IH*, 133)

It is possible to misunderstand Agamben's philosophical method by assuming that he tries to bring about a conscious historical development, wielding the magic wand of theory in order to transform one situation into another. For example, one might assume that his task in political philosophy is to pave the way for the transformation of what he calls "bare life" (the frog) into what he calls "form-of-life" (the prince). Like every fairy tale, Agamben's thought bears a certain promise of happiness. But before any life can be lived "happily ever after," or at least with some rudimentary sense of happiness, it must first "shake off the nightmare of myth," which Benjamin posits as the aim of every fairy tale (for example, when the fool intentionally "acts dumb" when confronted with a myth, or when the children see through the mythical forces that they used to fear so much).[21] Agamben identifies this nightmare as the myth of the sacredness of life. Here as elsewhere, it seems that an awakening can be achieved only by means of what Benjamin calls, quite enigmatically, "cunning" and "high spirits" (*Untermut* and *Übermut*, which both derive from *Mut*, or "courage").[22] For Adorno, by contrast, this awakening is only possible by means of a complex dialectical system of mediation between two neatly separated levels of existence, which he, like every good Marxist, calls "structure" and "superstructure." In our example, the maiden does not kiss the frog (which stands for all those concrete processes and material structures that fascinated Benjamin during his "micrological" work on the *Arcades Project*) because she conceives this deed as a means to an end, because she has in mind a sophisticated scheme that will eventually enable her to get hitched to the prince (who stands for the metaphysical totality or abstract and immaterial superstructure that Adorno demanded from Benjamin in their letter exchange from the winter of 1938). The maiden is neither a witch who knows how to transform one thing into another, nor is she the storyteller who is familiar with the whole narrative of the tale even before it is told, nor an interpreter who conjures up its allegorical meaning. Yet she still proves her unique cunning and high spirits as she (and no one else) musters the courage to kiss the frog-prince's lips. For Agamben, this kiss symbolizes a zone of indistinction that can undermine any attempt to separate not only humanity from animality but also culture from nature, form from matter, idea from fact, before from after. To those who contend, along with Adorno, that there is something vulgar about the absence of definitive separations or systematic causality between these two realms, Agamben retorts: "The fear of vulgarity betrays the vulgarity of fear" (*IH*, 131). By making immediate or unmediated links between singular elements from the structure and the superstructure, Benjamin does not practice vulgar materialism but a courageous one.

The kiss in this fairy tale certainly demands a more clear-headed explanation, as it is far from being an accidental gesture in Agamben's thought. In fact, it may even serve as the most helpful metaphor for his own brand of dialectics at a standstill. To see this point, consider one of the most celebrated kisses in the history of modern literature, which takes place at the end of "The Grand Inquisitor," the central parable in Dostoevsky's *Brothers Karamazov*.[23] The first curious thing that I should mention about this parable is that Ivan Karamazov insists on calling it a *poem*, although it is conveyed in simple prose. According to this prose-poem, Christ returns to Spain in the sixteenth century, performs a few miracles, and is adored by the people as the true Messiah. But before long the cynical Inquisition, which perceives Jesus as a threat to the status quo, decides to sentence him to death. Since Christ does not utter a word throughout the parable, the bulk of the (mainly existentialist) commentators focus on the long speech of the Grand Inquisitor during his nocturnal visit to the cell where the Resurrected awaits his execution. I would like to say nothing about this speech and focus entirely on Christ's reply, which Ivan recounts after Alyosha, his young brother, implores: "And how does your poem end?" It ends when the old inquisitor concludes his denunciation and Christ gently kisses him on his "bloodless" lips. A little later, Ivan, the archetypal atheist, wonders out loud whether he can still be embraced by his pious little brother after pronouncing his solidarity with the inquisitor's venomous speech. Instead of giving a verbal reply, Alyosha, the imitator of Christ, simply kisses his brother in silence.

I have mentioned that Ivan presents his parable as a poem because I was thinking about Agamben's claim that the end of the poem, the last line in every poetic composition, presents a puzzling difficulty. The only consistent criterion that may distinguish poetry from prose is the presence of enjambment, that is, the breaking of a syntactic unit between the poem's lines (for example, "The Radical Means" [break] Wasteland, but only to the eye [break] that serves life, [break] feather-light rubble"). Alternatively, we may say that enjambment does not break the sentence but inserts a brake in its midst. The difficulty arises from the fact that this definition cannot account for the poem's end. If a poem is founded on the tension between its metrical and syntactic elements, on the noncoincidence of sound and sense (which is the direct outcome of enjambment), then its end, from which enjambment is missing (because there is no further line to carry over the final idea), is what Agamben calls "the state of poetic emergency" (*EP*, 113). The last verse is the place where the tension generated by enjambment—this dialectical play of sound and sense, poetry and prose—is not resolved but arrives at a baffling stalemate.

This aporia reverberates in Arendt's invocation of the end of Dostoevsky's prose-poem as part of her attempt in *On Revolution* to explain her notion of compassion. One of her observations there is that com-passion, this shared suffering, tends to use a language of gestures rather than of words: "It is because he listens to the Grand Inquisitor's speech with compassion, and not for lack of arguments, that Jesus remains silent, struck, as it were, by the suffering which lay behind the easy flow of his opponent's great monologue. The intensity of this listening transforms the monologue into a dialogue, but it can be ended only by a gesture, the gesture of the kiss, not by words."[24] This kiss enables Arendt to reevaluate her cherished conception of the political as a space for discourse, since compassion abolishes the necessary distance between persons, whereas politics typically takes place through reasoning, arguments, calculations, persuasions, negotiations, compromises, and other (predominantly linguistic) apparatuses. The conclusion of Dostoevsky's aporetic poem, like every end of every poem according to Agamben, is therefore a zone in which language "collapses into silence" (*EP*, 115). This compassionate silence may very well mark the end of politics as we know it, or at least its suspension. But since such a compassionate silence can sometimes be infinitely more thoughtful than many of the banalities common in political discourse, it can also function as a symbolic beginning of the coming political life that operates within a dialectical standstill. That such a beginning is not so far off from what Nietzsche calls "the stillest hour" is evident from his oft-quoted (but not yet banal) claim that "it is the stillest words that bring on the storm. Thoughts that come on doves' feet guide the world."[25] Here is the same idea, now formulated as a Zen kōan: A master asks his student, "What is the stillest word?" In reply, the student gives his master a kiss.

Brachylogy

Following in Wittgenstein's footsteps, Agamben claims that philosophical prose must be "poeticized," or else it runs the risk of falling into banality, of lacking thought (*EP*, 115). This attitude partly explains the mosaic-like nature of his work. The tesserae that make up his texts are fragments chiseled from larger stones, or texts, written by others. It is a kind of historical materialism, not in the sense of a historical analysis directed at material processes but in the sense of a philosophical process that uses history as its material, indeed, as its capital, and thus wins over history itself by going against its grain. The resulting mosaic, however, is not a jigsaw puzzle, where simply putting the pieces in the right place will reveal a hidden, preordained picture. A preliminary name for this method might be *détournement*: the cutting, pasting, and altering of found materials in the process of creating a new work. The best example of this method can be found in Guy Debord's films (for instance, *The Society of the Spectacle* from 1973), which are made up of a montage of seemingly unrelated available images (commercials, newsreels, Hollywood films, pornographic images, etc.) and accompanied by a monologue written and recited by Debord himself. By appropriating what seems at times to be a bottomless cache of references rummaged from the archives of our tradition, Agamben performs what could be called a philosophical *détournement*. To go back for a moment to our earlier train analogy, we might also call it "historical derailment."

Agamben's texts offer various paths for possible struggles. An effective strategy of resistance, however, can no longer be restricted to a single plane of thought or action. Rather, it must branch out into what Deleuze and Guattari call "a thousand plateaus." Agamben's work, however, remains decidedly confined to the creation of *philological* plateaus. The favorite tools of his trade are quotations, which Benjamin describes as "wayside robbers who leap out, armed, and relieve the idle stroller of his conviction" (be aware, once again, that when writers misuse this tool, it is they, rather than their readers, who end up getting robbed of their own convictions).[26] Although a visual artist can use any sort of material, a writer has only sentences (as well as the occasional illustration), which are often treated by Agamben as "found objects." But it must be said that he is a philologist in the same way that Foucault is a historian. A citation, like the whole of the Western tradition, is not considered by Agamben to be authoritative, and he does not see himself as its heir. When he uses a quote, he always takes it "out of context," in the simple sense that he places it in the new context of his own work. Even though he never denies that the Western tradition is the very air that he breathes, his aim is not to evoke it in its petrified state or conform to it while it remains in force without significance. Instead, his books are basically meant to *make* the tradition with an evident dash of revolutionary violence. To borrow another expression from Benjamin, we could say that every quotation in Agamben's books aspires to be a *citation à l'ordre du jour*, a citation charged with an exigent demand that concerns the business of the day—and that day is always today.[27]

Though he usually immerses himself in meticulous and systematic scholarly studies, Agamben likes to present his findings in the form of miniature sketches, images, or scenes—each of which can stand both still and alone. When he collects these vignettes into a monograph, they sometimes resemble a flip book, which gives the fleeting illusion of a moving image by the quick turn of the pages with the thumb and index finger. In an interview from 1985 on the occasion of the publication of *Idea of Prose* (the book that best exemplifies his fragmentary style of writing), Agamben speaks about "brachylogy as a form of philosophy" without developing this idea any further.[28] Brachylogy comes from the Greek *brakhus* and *logos*, or "short speech." In modern languages, it stands for a concise form of speaking or writing that dispenses with conjunctives (as in newspaper headlines, which use brachylogy quite liberally). But if we consider this concept in logical rather than grammatical terms (grammar and logic are always very close to one another), brachylogy could also be said to stand for a form of philosophy without logical operations (*not, and, or, if/then*). This is not to claim that Agamben's work is illogical (compared with contemporary philosophy, both Continental and analytic, his writings are for the most part as clear as it gets) but rather that his thought does not pretend to lead us from point A to point B by means of an argumentative apparatus. Though he offers us rungs, they are not affixed to the two sidebars that would result in a ladder on which one could comfortably ascend or descend. Again, we note the futility in trying to speak about the progression of Agamben's "train of thought." His "operationless" philosophy at a standstill is consistent with his promotion of an "inoperative" way of thinking and living that suspends whatever end an idea, a thing, or an action was directed toward, and instead finds for it "a new possible use" (N, 102). In the same way, each of the rungs that composes Agamben's own philosophy can also be deactivated and reappropriated by his reader, by giving it a new context, a new application, a new life.

Bricolage

I would like now to suggest that "bricolage," rather than brachylogy, is another, even more appropriate name for Agamben's philosophical practice (any relation between the two terms appears to be accidental). The French *bricolage*, which is close to the English notion of "do it yourself," received its paradigmatic sense in "The Science of the Concrete," the opening chapter of Claude Lévi-Strauss's *The Savage Mind*. As the anthropologist tries to introduce his subject matter, he turns to a description of the *bricoleur*, a common French name for the amateur handyman who makes do with found instruments and materials, and contrasts him with the engineer. He explains that whereas the bricoleur improvises with whatever is at hand, the engineer specializes in a defined field that requires the availability of certain tools and raw materials. Where "the engineer is always trying to make his way out of and go beyond the constraints imposed by a particular state of civilization," Lévi-Strauss claims that "the bricoleur by inclination or necessity always remains within them."[29] If the engineer completes a "project" according to a plan and moves on to the next, "the bricoleur may not ever complete his purpose, but he always puts something of himself into it."[30] The motivation that leads Lévi-Strauss to make the distinction between the bricoleur and the engineer is not restricted to the technical realm. Bricolage is, after all, only his prefatory, descriptive name for a distinct way of thinking that is eventually defined in his book as "mythical" (an adjective that does not carry the same negative connotations we have seen Benjamin associating with it). It is also clear that the bricoleur and the mythical way of thinking are not simply meant to stand for the exotic mind of far-flung savages. It is no surprise, then, that since the publication of his book, bricolage and its Anglo-Saxon relative, "do it yourself," have served as models not only for new creative processes shared by many contemporary artists but also for an alternative way of life in late capitalism. Even though the term is not to be found in Benjamin's *Arcades Project* or Wittgenstein's *Philosophical Investigations* (both predate *The Savage Mind*), the practice of bricolage seems to be at play in these two unfinished masterpieces. It is only in Derrida's "Structure, Sign, and Play," and then in the opening chapter of Deleuze and Guattari's *Anti-Oedipus*, that the method of philosophical bricolage is invoked explicitly, if fleetingly. Taking its cue from this tradition, Agamben's work could be said to be a crystallization of the "science of the concrete" into a consistent and effective philosophical practice. The description of the bricoleur in *The Savage Mind* can thus provide a first account of the mind of a thinker (or a tinkerer) at a standstill—something Agamben's writings exemplify in a compelling way.

An intriguing account of the spirit of bricolage can be found in "The Ideal of the Broken," a short essay published in 1926 by the philosopher and economist Alfred Sohn-Rethel. Almost everything in Naples, Sohn-Rethel claims, is broken. In fact, the Neapolitans prefer to *begin* using their devices only *after* they break down and lose their original purpose. In Naples, an intact mechanism is seen as deeply uncanny and is viewed with great suspicion. A new machine first needs to be misused, then to malfunction, then to be fixed or altered in a makeshift way, and then, only then, can it really start to work. Notice, by the way, that this is a curious reversal of Heidegger's famous (though at the time still to be written) argument: whereas in *Being and Time* we are not supposed to notice the doorknob that we turn on a daily basis until it breaks and becomes what he calls "present-at-hand," the Neapolitans consider the moment at which a thing malfunctions as the moment when it can finally become "ready-to-hand." (Sohn-Rethel actually reports that doors are rarely left shut in Naples, so doorknobs are considered to be merely ornamental.) Here lies a unique answer to the question concerning technology: "The essence of technology," Sohn-Rethel concludes, "lies in making that which is broken function. In the handling of defunct mechanisms [the Neapolitan] is admittedly sovereign over all technology, and far beyond."[31] In Naples, it becomes very difficult to distinguish between use and misuse, function and malfunction, proper and improper. As Agamben suggests in a couple of passing comments on this essay, even the simple distinction between living beings and inanimate objects seems to break down, which leads to a new technical ability that "begins only when man is able to oppose the blind and hostile automatism of the machines."[32] In his own essay on Naples, written a year before Sohn-Rethel's, Benjamin also observes that "porosity is the inexhaustible law of life in this city, reappearing everywhere."[33] But the question persists: How should we understand the significance of these observations when we shift our focus from the technical plane to the intellectual one?

Ingenium

Two centuries before Sohn-Rethel, the Neapolitan philosopher Giambattista Vico became dissatisfied with the Cartesian school of thought that dominated the intellectual circles in which he moved. In *On the Most Ancient Wisdom of the Italians,* he claims that what those dogmatic Cartesians are lacking is *ingenium,* which is normally translated as "ingenuity," "inventiveness," or "mother wit." One may also recall at this point what Benjamin calls cunning and high spirits. Without *ingenium,* a philosopher may still be considered a decent craftsman (or, in Lévi-Strauss's terms, a good engineer), but nothing more. Vico's complaint is that the geometrical method deployed in the production of the typical philosophical tracts of his time could make a person go "mad rationally" when applied to practical life.[34] This, however, is far from being a superfluous criticism of a disgruntled thinker. Vico takes the notion of *ingenium* very seriously, defining it as "the faculty that connects disparate and diverse things," and claiming that imagination is in a sense the "eye" of *ingenium*.[35] For example, those who lack *ingenium* are absolutely blind to metaphors, similes, analogies, illustrations, allegories, and associations—which might not be the bread of philosophy, but they are certainly its butter (the reader will surely have noticed that this chapter is quite heavy on the latter). So while Descartes focuses on how we discover the truth by using our reason, Vico emphasizes the way in which we also *make* the truth through *ingenium*. This, in a nutshell, is his famous equation of *verum* and *factum*, that "the true is precisely what is made."[36]

Ingenium, Agamben reminds us, is closely linked to the word *genius*. The Romans believed that Genius was the name of a special god, born together with each and every human being. Birthday gifts and parties were originally dedicated to Genius. (Agamben makes a point in telling us that these traditionally included "incense, wine, and delicious honey cake, because Genius, the god who presides over birth, did not like blood sacrifices" [*P*, 9].) Although Genius was one's personal god, it is still not exactly one's self. It is, rather, an alterity of sorts. "Genius," Agamben writes, "is our life insofar as it does not belong to us" (*P*, 13). In this way, he places the ego of a person on one side, while positioning Genius on the opposite, impersonal, side. He claims that "the two forces coexist, intersect, separate, but can neither emancipate themselves completely from each other nor identify with each other perfectly" (*P*, 13). For Agamben, Ego and Genius constitute a bipolar opposition, while the subject dwells in their midst, constantly negotiating its position in relation to these two opposing forces.

One can now see in a new light Vico's hostility toward "the Cartesians of the letter, not the spirit" of the early eighteenth century, who wanted to ground their philosophy solely on that which belonged to them—the certainty of their ego's existence—while failing to listen to their *ingenium*.[37] Unlike these Cartesians, Descartes himself never ignores the element in his life that does *not* belong to him. This is already clear from his first major (though unfinished) work, *Regulae ad directionem ingenii*. The generic translation, "Rules for the Direction of the Mind" (or *esprit* in French), completely misses the fact that the ultimate concern of the book is to find a way to direct or calibrate our *ingenium*. It is also not a coincidence that in the first *Meditation* Descartes calls his grand deceiver "genium aliquem malignum," "some evil genius," and distinguishes it from the benevolent god (in the spirit of the long-standing tradition that splits the single Genius of the Romans into a good genius and a bad genius, pushing each person either to salvation or to damnation).[38] We can therefore comfortably apply Agamben's approach to Descartes's thought, by placing ego at one pole and genius at its opposite pole. From this perspective, one may wonder whether the Archimedean point of modern philosophy is truly an immovable "I exist" or whether it is a field of tensions between ego and genius, reason and *ingenium*.

Breathless Lingering

This is not the first time that we have come across a "field of tensions" in Agamben's work, which is closely linked to what he also likes to call a zone of indistinction, a point of indifference, or a threshold. These are probably the most persistent tropes in his writings, and they more or less consist of the same fundamental gesture: the pitting of two concepts against each other, followed by the localization of a sort of whirlpool in their midst, which in turn is meant to undermine the original dualism. Despite his dazzling plethora of references and subject matter, it is hard to miss how this device rules the internal logic of Agamben's entire thought. This signature move is employed at every important juncture and with a growing frequency throughout his work, to the extent that if there could be said to be a minimalist movement in contemporary philosophy (as in late twentieth-century music or art), Agamben would be one of its leading practitioners.

Sometimes, however, the specters of structuralism lead his search for those bipolar distinctions—in which he believes that our culture is trapped—to look a little bit like a witch hunt. The presupposition that humans live in between opposite poles, of course, is one of the favorite targets of the so-called poststructuralists. Deleuze, for instance, points out that "opposition is not a maximum of difference but a minimum of repetition—a repetition reduced to two, echoing and returning on itself."[39] But instead of bypassing the "dualism machine" (a feat that Deleuze, like Foucault, actually manages quite impressively), Agamben's strategy is to invoke this apparatus time and again, to repeat it indefinitely, and then to find in each instance a way to *disable* the dichotomy through the presentation of the zone of its indetermination, where one pole cannot be distinguished from its opposite. His conviction is that virtually every important opposition that we can think of is today *irreparably lost*, that it is no longer possible to clearly draw a separating line, and that our only option is to learn to inhabit the threshold, in between whatever division may come our way. This point of indifference, however, is not a place for unity, reconciliation, synthesis, fusion of horizons, or all-embracing tolerance, where the opposing poles somehow come to coincide. The alternative to dualism is not exactly monism. Since every undecidable threshold stands between accepted truths, traditional values, or fixed substances, we would miss the point if we were to treat this threshold as the new metaphysical truth, value, or substance of our culture. Agamben therefore insists on the *noncoincidence* of every opposition: he does not let the division collapse into itself by keeping it in a state of limbo, by maintaining it as an "uncertain terrain" (*ME*, 139). At one point he calls this field of tensions "a battlefield between irreconcilable demands," though he then goes on to describe this battle as an "amorous fight" (*EP*, 59). His zones of indistinction are therefore not exactly war zones between enemies but more like domestic quarrels between lovers, perhaps like the one between Zarathustra and Life.

"In Playland" is an early essay in which Agamben offers his most explicit meditation on the structuralist tradition. By developing the theme that concludes Lévi-Strauss's "The Science of the Concrete," Agamben distinguishes between the function of ritual, which is meant to solidify history and culture, and the function of play, which is meant to liquefy them: "while rites transform events into structures, play transforms structures into events" (*IH*, 82). In a more recent essay he adds that whereas a ritual is an act of consecration (that is, transforming what is profane into a sacred, separated object), play is an act of profanation (transforming the sacred object into something profane, thus bringing it back to everyday human use) (*P*, 73–76). Despite what might be expected, Agamben does not try to lead humanity through the gate of Playland, this place where all the solid structures that constitute our society melt away into timeless events. Rather, his consistent point is that rite and play complement one another and work together as a single mechanism. One can still distinguish between what Lévi-Strauss calls "cold" societies (where the tendency toward ritual is stronger) and "hot" societies (where the element of play has the upper hand). But a society of pure events (a life without form) or pure structures (a form without life) is not really livable. The only space in which humans can coexist remains this fracture between sacred ritual and profane play, this disjunction of "cold" structures and "hot" events, this field of tensions between rule and exception. Our only dwelling place, our ethos, where a form of life can thrive, is therefore always a kind of "laceration that is also a suture," a sort of "tension that is both the articulation of a difference and a unity" (*S*, 157). It is, in other words, the elementary manifestation of Agamben's dialectics at a standstill.

On the face of it, Agamben asks us to live a paradox, as opposing forces demand to take possession of our thoughts and actions, without ever resolving the matter in either direction. It seems that we can live, like Humpty Dumpty, only on the narrow wall that separates two established realms, though it is important to remember that, at least in Lewis Carroll's version, Humpty Dumpty neither falls nor cracks. One illuminating example of this condition at work is the adage *festina lente*, which is nicely translated as "excited delay" or "breathless lingering" (*EP*, 47). It is also beautifully illustrated by the frontispiece of Agamben's *Idea of Prose*, which reproduces an image of Eros riding on a snail (*IP*, iii). The scholar's form of life is charged with precisely this oxymoronic tension: on the one hand, there is always a sense of deferral, a feeling that, in regard to study, there is no end in sight; on the other hand, every research must also contain (at least the desire for) a distinct promise or closure. There seems to be a straight path, but there are always endless diversions and bypasses, which lend every good investigation the air of a *"euphoric* aporia" (Greek for "felicitous way" and "lack of way" [*PC*, 217]). This may have to do with Agamben's belief that only those who have no path will reach their end. As a result, the impression that we know what needs to be done endlessly oscillates between certainty and uncertainty, leading and being led, patience and impatience. One may also describe this condition as a "studious play" or playful study (*SE*, 64). Interestingly, Agamben treats "this shuttling between bewilderment and lucidity, discovery and loss, between patient and agent" as a sort of *rhythm* (*IP*, 64). According to his analysis, structure in its original sense is a kind of rhythm, rather than a scheme, which introduces into the "eternal flow a split and a stop" (*MC*, 99). For this reason he puts so much emphasis on Hölderlin's delirious exclamation: "Everything is rhythm, the entire destiny of man is one heavenly rhythm" (*MC*, 94). Through the very repetition of the signature gestures in his writings, Agamben produces an unmistakable rhythm that permeates his form of thinking and living. This observation may also finally help us to broach the difficulty in categorizing his philosophy as either pessimistic or optimistic. Somehow, it manages to dance to the beat of both drums, to oscillate between the two while giving in to neither (but also without appearing detached from either). This comportment is summed up in a remark that Agamben appropriated from Debord, who in turn appropriated it from Marx: "The desperate situation of society in which I live fills me with hope."[40]

The Philosopher and the Dog

Hans-Georg Gadamer ridicules those whom he considers to be acting like a dog that bites the master's pointing finger rather than look in the direction that it indicates.[41] This is a fine analogy, but it may also be easily turned against itself, because it now appears that it is actually the philosopher, rather than the dog, who might be misguided here. According to Agamben, if someone points in the direction to which we need to go, it is our prerogative to *bite the finger* (*PC*, 56). If people try to save us, we had better tell them that "there is nothing to save" (*CC*, 6). It is true that humans remain, in this sense, broken, like a train that comes to a standstill, like the ruins of an old building, like an incarcerated Christ, like the motor of a defunct motorbike that revolves, on a slightly crooked axis, in order to whip the cream in a Neapolitan dairy shop. But precisely because we are irremediable or unredeemable, exactly because our mending (what in Lurianic Kabbalah is called *tiqqun*) is never complete, we live a life that is truly and fully immersed in ethical and political questions. The attempts to fight against this irreparable and imperfect human condition by consigning man to a universal truth, by giving him a historical or spiritual vocation, by grounding him in a defined essence, by fitting him into a fixed narrative, by directing him toward an original unity, or by assuring him a particular destiny, are all based on a common insidious aim: to run both ethics and politics into the ground, because then all that will be left for humanity to do is to follow the user manual that came in the box shipped from the philosopher's factory.

Nevertheless, Agamben assures us that the rejection of the tendency to follow the pointing finger "does not mean that, in lacking an end, [humans] are condemned to meaninglessness or the vanity of an infinite, disenchanted drifting. They have not an *end*, but a *remnant*. There is no foundation in or beneath them; rather, at their center lies an irreducible disjunction in which each term, stepping forth in the place of a remnant, can bear witness" (*RA*, 159). Instead of being defined, life always breaks down and divides itself. Humans tend to repress this fact by seeing themselves as in-dividuals (that is to say, indivisible) or by thinking about themselves as parts of some unified whole. To be a remnant is to resist this totalizing tendency by always bearing witness to the differences that separate us from each other and by never letting go of the divisions that split each one of us from within. Given the liberal attempt to achieve complete reconciliation, the conservative effort to maintain a clear distinction, the chauvinist affirmation of one side, and the antipathetic rejection of the other, Agamben's use of the enigmatic notion of the remnant leads him toward a positive vision of human beings as, so to speak, walking oxymorons, living aphorisms, a community of fragments, who have no need of coinciding with a coherent universal whole, or even with their very own selves. After so many philosophers have tried to eat humanity's cake and keep it whole, Agamben has realized that the only ethical or political consistency that makes sense today is that of the crumb, the leftover, the remnant. "If man is that which may be *infinitely* destroyed," he therefore writes, "this also means that something other than this destruction, and within this destruction, remains, and that man is the remnant" (*TR*, 53). Like unfinished manuscripts, human beings are open-ended; they never stop reading what remains to be written in the incomplete book of life.

Present While Absent

The Politics of Presence

The ultimate task of Western metaphysics since the time of the Greeks has been to comprehend the single essence behind the multitude of concrete beings, to distill from the term "being" (which, Aristotle observes, is "said in many ways") a sort of "pure Being" (*on haplōs*).[1] Nevertheless, Heidegger tells us, this task remained concealed for millennia, so in the beginning of *Being and Time* he calls upon us "to raise anew the question of the meaning of Being," which he presents as "*the* fundamental question of philosophy."[2] In a barely disguised similar vein, Agamben describes "the separation of bare life from the many forms of concrete life" as the fundamental, though once again hidden, task of Western politics. Life, which, according to Aristotle, is also "said in many ways," is revealed in *Homo Sacer* to be the very thing that politics incessantly seeks to capture and reduce to a bare life, to the mere fact of being alive.[3] From this perspective, the horizons of politics and metaphysics may look as if they merge, which leads Agamben to wonder: "Pure Being, bare life—what is contained in these two concepts, such that both the metaphysics and the politics of the West find their foundation and sense in them and in them alone? What is the link between the two constitutive processes by which metaphysics and politics seem, in isolating their proper element, simultaneously to run up against an unthinkable limit?" (*HS*, 182).

The not-so-secret affinity between Being and living (which extends at least from Aristotle's "Being, for the living, is life," to Nietzsche's "Being—we have no other way of imagining it apart from 'living'") constitutes the ground for an extremely suggestive alliance between biopolitics and metaphysics.[4] This clarifies, first of all, why now is the time to raise anew the question of the meaning of living, rather than of Being, as the true fundamental question of philosophy. (For Agamben, however, it is not the existentialist quest for the meaning of life, but the structuralist search for the form of life, which stands at the center of his thought.) More to the point, if the discussion in the past century about the "end of metaphysics" had any merit, could we also arrive in our century at some sort of "end of biopolitics," at least as we know it? Or is it better to come to terms with the history of metaphysics in such a way that a new image of the political will consequently come to life? But how can we approach these two disciplines without eventually reaching the very problematic notions of pure Being and bare life? Perhaps we should not renounce the similar horizons of the two traditions but instead follow Agamben in his attempt to think them through all the way to their extreme, where they indeed seem to collapse into one another: "Brought to the limit of pure Being, metaphysics (thought) passes over into politics (into reality), just as on the threshold of bare life, politics steps beyond itself into theory" (HS, 182).

Not to discount Agamben's own attempts to approach and reproach the metaphysico-political linkage, in what follows I will trace an aspect of this connection that may be found in fragments of ideas scattered throughout his work, though they never came together to form an integrated approach. To begin, let us turn to what he considers "the first recording of bare life as the new political subject," which also happens to be "the document that is generally placed at the foundation of modern democracy: the 1679 writ of *habeas corpus*" (HS, 123). The central idea expressed in this cherished text is that a person should not be absent from the court in which he is being accused. Agamben, however, shows that the person at the center of this seemingly enlightened writ is not really treated as a person at all. Instead, he is simply called "*Corpus X*," or "body X, by whatsoever name he may be called" (HS, 123–24). The true political subject reveals itself for the first time to be neither a free man nor a citizen but just an anonymous body. Though in modern politics this bare life constitutes the substance that is the bearer of liberties and rights (and thus it is ordinarily cared for and protected from peril), it is also the ultimate target of power and law (and thus it can potentially be forsaken and harmed).

Whereas Agamben focuses his analysis of habeas corpus on the issue of the body, I would like to shift the emphasis to the closely related question of presence: the insistence that body X must be shown in front of the court, that it ought to be *physically present* while its fate is being determined. The decisive point, after all, is not only that the accused is considered to be a body but that the court, that the law, demands to "have" this body (habeas corpus literally means "you shall have the body"). It would be worthwhile, then, to investigate this strange desire of the state to obtain an immediate access not only to the body of the person on trial but essentially to any member of the body politic. We all have some personal familiarity with those awkward moments at a border or police checkpoint, at an army draft office or a Social Security office, during an election or a census, when a baby is born or a person dies, when we can literally sense the unmediated contact between this or that apparatus of power (which usually leaves the "good citizens" alone) and this or that bare life. In such moments we tend to feel accused even though we have not done anything wrong. The familiar experience of being-in-the-world is easily reduced to being-in-the-Israeli-checkpoint-at-the-entrance-to-Bethlehem, being-in-the-office-of-the-New-York-City-clerk-for-a-marriage-license, and so forth.

The rather expansive question that I would now like to explore is whether this line of investigation could help us understand something elemental about Western politics, in the same way that a similar approach enabled Jacques Derrida to see Western metaphysics as the tradition that cannot escape from thinking about Being as something that is primarily present, and thus to overlook the importance of that which is absent. Could we learn to critique the "politics of presence" in the same way that we used to critique the "metaphysics of presence"? And if so, how are we then going to pose the question of living, like the question of Being, without surrendering to the temptation of answering it in the pervasive vocabulary of presence? What sense can we still make of the ancient Greeks' demand that it must be possible to take in the entire population of a state with a single sweeping glance or to address it with a single booming voice, which cannot be completely fulfilled in the modern state even with the proliferation of surveillance cameras and television sets?[5] Is it possible to think today about political action without resorting to the Greek agora and the Roman forum, or their pale modern replicas in various houses of "re-present-atives," along with all those attempts to compensate for the adulteration of pure politics through the march, the demonstration, or the sit-in, where the question of presence is virtually inescapable?

Derrida traces the origin of the metaphysics of presence to the tendency to think about language first and foremost as speech, in which the present voice of a spoken word can directly correspond to some present entity. We perceive writing, however, to be secondary to speaking, like a trace of something that is no longer there. For example, I look outside my window and say, "Now it is night." I then write this truism down in an e-mail to a friend. But what is the status of this same sentence once it is read after a good night's sleep, or in a different time zone? A decisive part of Derrida's strategy is to try to overcome the metaphysics of presence by reversing this traditional picture, by considering writing (*gramma* in Greek), instead of speaking, as the primary phenomenon (and thus he calls his approach "grammatology"). In this way, the written sentence about the night gains a life of its own, without being shackled to the night itself. Rather than think about the trace as a failure to correspond to something that is not present, try to think about the trace as the thing itself, and let the whole question of presence dissipate. On this ground, we can again see why the question of Being is so close to the question of living. When Derrida first introduces the metaphysics of presence in *Speech and Phenomena*, he does not fail to criticize it as a philosophy of *life*, since our idea of presence depends on what he calls "the living present," whereas speaking is always understood as a "living speech."[6] "Life," he can therefore conclude, "must be thought of as trace before Being may be determined as presence."[7] Without our making this move, the basic matrix of metaphysics (and thus politics) cannot be overcome.

There is, however, a slight problem with this strategy. If Heidegger conceived the history of metaphysics as a perpetual blindness to the question of Being, and Derrida held that the same tradition is oblivious to the problem of presence, then the next step becomes rather predictable. Derrida, Agamben claims, "believed he had opened a way to surpass metaphysics, while in truth he merely brought its fundamental problem to light" (*LD*, 39). Agamben's main claim is that even our viva voce, the speech uttered by the voice of a living being, which is supposed, *pace* Derrida, to offer us an unmediated access to things, to presence, *is already a trace*. As we saw earlier, Agamben shows that at the origin of Western thought there is never a true presence but always an absence, a negative foundation, an empty space. Speech is therefore not so different from writing: the former, like the latter, is grounded in what is ultimately ungrounded; its basis is always a void. Ultimately, the voice is an index that points to silence, and *metaphysics is from the beginning nothing but grammatology*. This place of negativity at the heart of metaphysics finds its perfect parallel in Agamben's understanding of the place of sacrifice at the heart of politics: the *exclusion* of the sacred man from the community, the *absence* of bare life from the political realm (along with the empty center where we expect to find the sovereign), becomes today, according to this analysis, the unthinkable limit—which is also the very foundation—of the dysfunctional society in which we live.

The Spiral of the Possible

The outcome of the previous deliberations is clearly an aporia: neither the metaphysics of presence criticized by Derrida nor the metaphysics of absence that is the aim of Agamben's own critique could function as the basis for the coming politics. At best, they help us better understand the double trap that we need to avoid. But to see how this can be done, we need to make a short digression.

The Trading with the Enemy Act, which came into effect across the realm of the declining British Empire in 1939, gave the Crown's custodian the legal right to claim as his own the property of those who fled their homes and lands during wartime and failed to return afterward. The act extinguishes the rights of the former owners, who are deemed in absentia as "enemies," even though they are, in most cases, harmless refugees. The veiled implication of this provision was a suspension of the principle established by the habeas corpus writ. The empire can decide to take your land without your consent and, most important, without your ability to argue otherwise in front of a court of law.[8]

The Israeli Declaration of Independence from the British Empire in 1948 led to a war between the Jews and the Arabs that concluded, a year later, with the victory of the former. Shortly after, as the new Jewish state began to consolidate its legal system on the basis of the British one, the Trading with the Enemy Act proved to be extremely useful, albeit with a decisive alteration. The Palestinians who fled their villages during the war but returned after the battles subsided were rather surprised to discover that the Israeli army had taken full control of their property. The authorities told them that even though they were indeed "present" within the boundaries of the Israeli territories, as far as their lands, homes, shops, bank accounts, stocks, artworks, and so forth were at stake, they were considered "absentees." Though these "internal refugees" were physically present in the courtrooms where they repeatedly appealed to reclaim what was previously theirs, in the eyes of the law they were, at the very same time, absent. In official legal documents they were therefore referred to—with what must be one of the most colossal disregards of basic common sense in the history of jurisprudence—as "present-absentees."[9]

In 1992, before the so-called peace process between the Israelis and the Palestinians was revealed to the public, the writer David Grossman found a new use for this paradoxical piece of legalese. He transformed it into an illuminating metaphor not only for those Arabs whose property was taken from them after the 1948 war but for all the Palestinians who have lived since then within the boundaries of the Israeli state.[10] Those "present-absent" people, he noticed, live in a strange state of suspension: they cannot be confused with their Palestinian brothers and sisters who have lived under martial law in the territories occupied by the Israeli army since the 1967 war, but they also fundamentally differ from the Jewish citizens who have lived under ordinary law since the 1948 war. Even though those Israeli-Palestinians are citizens, they are to this day both de facto and de jure "second-class" citizens in many respects.

To return to Agamben's terminology, we may say that those present-absentees occupy the threshold between, on the one hand, the precarious bare lives of the Arab men, women, and children who live in a permanent state of exception within the occupied territories, and, on the other hand, the comfortable form of life of the Jewish "full" citizens who live under normal civil law. Let us therefore divide the population into three very schematic groups: the Israelis are "present-present," the Palestinians are "absent-absent," and the Israeli-Palestinians are "present-absent."

The utopia of modern politics consists of present-present people, with equal rights from the state and full protection under the law. The dystopia, as Agamben describes it, consists of absent-absent people, bare lives, sacred men, with neither rights nor protection. In both models, the present-absent people would be considered transitory figures, on the way either to their redemption or to their damnation. But I would now like to diverge from this line of thinking. I want to ask whether the threshold between the polar opposites of pure presence and pure absence may enable us to bring to a standstill this tired dialectics that has plagued our metaphysico-political way of thinking and living. I wonder whether those present-absent people—because of (rather than despite) the deep ambivalence that permeates their everyday lives, and without ever forgetting their suffering—could be conceived as the true vanguard of a community still to come. What we are dealing with here is far more than a bizarre legal status. We may expand the present-absent condition to encompass anyone who, by choice or by necessity, partakes *and* abstains, is included *and* excluded, is there *and* not there, when a certain place, rule, institution, association, occupation, culture, language, or practice is at stake. It is even possible to consider presence-absence as a fundamental mood or comportment, a powerful strategy or tactic, which can be detected virtually anywhere we turn in today's world: not only, therefore, refugees, denizens, and immigrants but also those who operate on the fringes of a profession, a society, or an organization; those who constantly move in between multiple locations, vocations, or identities; those "netizens" who, for hours on end, surf the Internet; those who lose themselves in reading and writing; and so on. Like guests or travelers, such present-absent people never feel that they completely belong, as they always make sure to qualify their presence with a healthy dose of absence. It seems safe to say that everyone is present-absent to a certain degree in certain situations or certain times. It is even possible to claim that while "to be or not to be" might still be considered the question, "to be *and* not to be" is probably one of the better answers that we can give. This is a good way to approach what Agamben means by the term "potentiality," which, he claims, is "not simply non-Being, simple privation, but rather *the existence of non-Being*, the presence of an absence" (*PC*, 179). This is the reason he claims that it is only "on the threshold between Being and non-Being" that one can find "the luminous spiral of the possible" (*PC*, 257).

Both presence and absence, in their unadulterated forms, are *myths* that modern political thought cannot help accepting. Yet it appears that there is a possible third way. An interesting example of this approach may be found in Benedict Anderson's definition of the nation as "an imagined political community": it is "imagined" because its members "will never know most of their fellow members," even though "in the minds of each lives the image of their communion," which means that the nation can still be considered a community because it is "always conceived as a deep, horizontal comradeship."[11] Since the idyllic immediate presence of all the community members in the same classical agora or the same medieval village or the same modern commune is no longer feasible today, the nation must manufacture (in intricate ways that Anderson and others enumerate) a sense of togetherness, of a shared origin, ground, and destiny, which allows all the members of a particular nation-state to perceive themselves and each other as, for example, "Italian," or "American." One problem with Anderson's thesis, which is actually its hidden virtue, is that there is no apparent reason why an imagined community needs to be dependent on the state apparatus. Isn't it also possible to speak about "nonsovereign imagined communities" that are not restricted to the boundaries of nations but are simply understood as forms of life? As a preliminary example, can't we think about Judaism during the nearly two millennia spent as the Diaspora (which is to say, before and after it was associated with a certain territorial state) as such an imagined community or a form of life? Other tentative examples may be modern groups like the proletariat, international businessmen, soccer fans, computer hackers, graffiti artists, sadomasochists, or Agamben readers: can't they also be conceived as constituting imagined communities that intersect here and there with this or that state but ultimately transcend it? And what about the community of philosophers, this strange form of life that seems to be present as much as it is absent? "In a sense," Agamben muses, "philosophy is scattered in every territory. It is always a diaspora, and must be recollected and gathered up."[12] To pose the question in geographical terms, it seems appropriate to ask whether there is still any reason to think about a "living space," the infamous Nazi lebensraum, as a simple physical territory possessed by a well-defined national group, or to which the national group makes claims. Without trying to sound too lofty, I wonder whether the truly powerful living space today is in fact an imaginary space (or maybe even a "virtual" one, in Deleuze's sense of the word), in which living beings are simultaneously present and absent.[13] Anyone who is interested in a more in-depth investigation into this set of questions should consult *Stanzas*, Agamben's early study of the medieval notion of "phantasm," its links to the modern concept of imagination, and its function as *the medium between the corporeal and the incorporeal*.[14] One may also recall in this context Kant's idea that the faculty of imagination is what enables us *to make present what is absent*.[15] By taking this route, we can better understand what it takes to *imagine* a form of life. "Whoever seizes the greatest unreality," Hugo von Hofmannsthal suggests in a similar spirit, "will shape the greatest reality."[16]

Heraclitus compares those who fail to comprehend what they have heard to people who are deaf: they have ears, but they cannot hear. He then uses a common Greek saying to deride such people by calling them "present while absent" (*pareontas apeinai*).[17] Even though they appear to be physically present, their failure to grasp the *logos* deems them absent in Heraclitus's eyes. This pejorative use of the present-absent condition makes perfect sense within the context of Greek political society, where every citizen was expected to show his full presence in the public realm (remember, however, that women, slaves, children, and foreigners were considered to be simultaneously present in and absent from the polis). The fact that today we understand this ancient saying exactly as the Greeks used to understand it proves something about our shared political sensibilities. It is, perhaps, only on the day when Heraclitus's reference to those who are present while absent will no longer carry the same derogatory sense in the mind of his future readers (so a footnote will need to be inserted in order to dispel the confusion) that this ancient pattern of thought will no longer haunt our own, and the door to a new politics will be cracked open at last.

I Am Whatever I Am

By returning now to Agamben's terminology, we may further characterize the present-absent being as a "whatever being." In order to understand this essential idea in Agamben's thought, let us turn to the medieval Jewish philosopher Levi ben Gershon's neat solution to the great scandal of epistemology: the false need to choose between the universal and the particular. Consider, for example, the word *dog*. Why is this concept intelligible for you? Is it that you think about some universal definition of *dog*, which is then applied to every possible entity that answers to this general criterion? Or is it that you think about all the actual individual dogs that you have encountered in the world, which in turn constitute your unified and abstract concept of "dog"? The answer, ben Gershon claims, is neither. You do not induce from the particular up to the universal, nor do you deduce from the universal down to the particular. Instead, he suggests, you simply think about *whatever* dog you happen to entertain in your mind.[18] "In this conception," Agamben explains, "such-and-such being is reclaimed from its having this or that property, which identified it as belonging to this or that set, to this or that class (the reds, the French, the Muslims)" (CC, 1). Instead, it now becomes possible to perceive a being without relying on the jargon of particulars and universals, but simply by conceiving it *as such*, as a *whatever singularity*.

Agamben offers further illustrations of this strange condition of whateverness that are worth recounting. The first one is love. My love cannot be directed at a particular property of a person, since then it would be no more than a fixation (I love only brunettes with curly hair) or a rationalization (I love her because she is a brunette with curly hair). But my love cannot neglect such properties, because if it did, it would become an insipid universal love (I love whomever; it does not really matter). Love does not, or at least should not, play the overly simplistic logical game of universals versus particulars (I am capable of loving only men; Socrates is a man; hence I can fall in love with Socrates). Instead, try to think about the "whatever singularity" of the one you love. "The lover," Agamben writes, "wants the loved one *with all its predicates*, its being such as it is . . . the *as* insofar as it is *such*" (*CC*, 2). Love is therefore understood as the ability to conceive someone, or maybe even something, "simply in its being-thus—irreparable, but not for that reason necessary; thus, but not for that reason contingent" (*CC*, 106).

Another helpful illustration of "whateverness" is handwriting. The idiosyncratic way by which you write the letter *p* can be distinguished (at least by a good graphologist) from a thousand other exemplars. Nevertheless, anyone can understand your singular handwritten *p* as the common sign *p* (unless you are a physician writing a prescription). The ability of your script to be both individual and generic is what deems it in Agamben's eyes as "whatever." To be a whatever being is to embrace this oscillation between the poles of the abstract structure of language and its real manifestation, the universal and the particular, the potential and the actual. The manner in which such a whatever being "passes from the common to the proper and from the proper to the common is called usage—or rather, *ethos*" (*CC*, 20). It is, in other words, a form of life, which is always shared by different whatever singularities. Agamben's point, therefore, is not that we need to do away with all classes or identities (the fact that I am a woman, Buddhist, lesbian) by repressing or dissipating or transcending them. Since no identity is sacred, the ethical task is actually to profane it, use it, play with it, examine it, struggle for and against it, or even render it completely inoperative within our life, but without trying to resolve the matter once and for all. A whatever singularity may accept and reject the same identity or shuttle between a number of identities. Rather than being *x* (insert here your identity of choice), try to be and not to be *x*. This, in a nutshell, is how "identity politics" may become "whatever politics," or even "form of life politics."

There is, however, another manifestation of "whatever being" (in fact, its ultimate manifestation) about which Agamben prefers to remain silent. During Moses's first encounter with God (who was speaking to him from a burning bush) the former cautiously poses to the latter an indirect and hypothetical question: Suppose that the people would ask me for your name, what then should I tell them? God answers: "Eheya asher eheye," which is traditionally translated as "I am who I am," after the Latin *Ego sum qui sum* (Exodus 3:14). Agamben mentions that this tautological proposition is considered to be the closest that one could ever get to the meaning of the tetragram YHVH, the explicit name of the Jewish God that can only be written but never said (*LD*, 30). This connection is extremely important for ontology, because what is at stake in both the tautology and the tetragram is the very question of Being (*havaya* in Hebrew). With this in mind, Agamben evokes Maimonides's suggestion that the mysterious doubling in "I am who I am"—where "the object which is to be described and the attribute by which it is described are in this case necessarily identical"—indicates that, in God, existence (that he is) and essence (what he is) coincide without leaving any residue (*SL*, 52). Agamben does not mention, however, that Spinoza (for whom God's essence always involves existence), considers YHVH as a unique contraction of the three tenses of the verb "to be" (I am, I was, I will be) into a single name.[19] He elaborates this idea in a letter dated from June 1666: "Since God's nature does not consist in one definite kind of being, but in being which is absolutely indeterminate, his nature also demands all that which perfectly expresses being; otherwise his nature would be determinate and deficient."[20] From this perspective, the question *qui est* (who is), when referred to God, can only be answered by *quodlibet est* (whatever is). I would thus like to suggest an alternative translation of God's reply to Moses, which seems to be both quite similar to, and very different from, the usual one. Not "I am who I am," but "I am *whatever* I am." The question, then, is, can the divine essence of God, what the onto-theological tradition calls "pure Being," be in any way distinguished from the everyday, earthly existence of Agamben's "whatever being"? And isn't God the exemplary Being that is both present *and* absent?

Not unlike the life of God, the life of man is a zone of indetermination that is "said in many ways." A human being is therefore conceived in Agamben's philosophy as "the living being that has no specific nature and vocation," as the form of life that no particular work or destiny can exhaust.[21] If humans learn to lead their lives as present-absent whatever singularities, it will become very difficult, if not impossible, to subsume them under a predetermined class, group, concept, or identity. The problem, however, is that in our culture it is still difficult for some to realize that "whateverness" is a blessing and not a curse, that this condition can empower rather than weaken our way of being. Consider, for example, the Heideggerian orthodoxy, which considers life to be "hazy," as "constantly being re-enshrouded in fog."[22] This view is crucial to the argument of *Being and Time*, in which the concept of life is systematically disregarded as "undetermined."[23] *Unbestimmtheit* is usually translated as "indetermination," though it is also possible to render it as "indecision" or "uncertainty." But what is most interesting about this word is its connection to such crucial Heideggerian notions as *stimmung* (mood), *stimmen* (tuned), and *stimme* (voice). From this perspective, the strategy of Heidegger's book is to find a way to determine human life in an ontological manner by means of the new term "Dasein" in order to give this life a decisive voice, to put it in a certain mood, to ensure that it will no longer be out of tune with Being. Nevertheless, it is important to note, as Jean-Luc Marion does, that the key sections in the book dedicated to anxiety, death, and the call are precisely the moments when Dasein finds itself in an indecisive state of being.[24] Without those three uncertain terrains, Dasein's eventual and overall ontological determination would simply be inconceivable. It is therefore not so surprising to hear the young Heidegger, five years before the publication of his magnum opus, telling his students that the "indeterminateness of the object, 'my life,' is not a defect"; that "this indeterminateness points out the object and yet does not predetermine it"; that regarding the notion of life, "we merely play with the term—or, rather, it is this term that plays with the philosopher."[25] He therefore gives an ominous warning about the day when the intention to grasp the concept of life will be "abandoned, and this abandonment [will be] justified on the grounds that life is ambiguous and therefore impossible to understand clearly and precisely. Yet the height of indolence, and the bankruptcy of philosophy, consists in the plea that the term is not to be used at all. We thereby avoid a troublesome admonition—and write a system."[26] Though Heidegger seems to be criticizing here the mature Hegel for betraying his youthful philosophy of life, the development of Heidegger's own work shows that he could not help making this same dubious move.

Becoming Imperceptible

"The novelty of the coming politics," Agamben declares, "is that it will no longer be a struggle for the conquest or control of the state, but a struggle between the state and the non-state (humanity), an insurmountable disjunction between whatever singularity and the state organization" (CC, 85). In other words, he does not want to claim that the misty terrain of Whateverland has the rigid consistency of a new sovereign state. The hope is that by insisting on our whatever singularities, we will no longer be an easy target for the state and, it must be added, the corporation. The powers that be must decide, define, and fixate our identities within particular groups and classes if they wish to effectively govern our bodies, control our actions, and manipulate our desires. If it is true that "visibility is a trap," as Foucault maintains, then being invisible may help us to become invincible, because power tends to fear a vacuum.[27] This means, to use Agamben's own terms, that the task is to expose "in every form one's own amorphousness and in every act one's own inactuality" (CC, 44). The guiding question of this formless form of life, or this inactive political activity, which is present but also absent, may thus be posed in the following way: How to disappear completely, or at least almost completely?

Agamben's early studies often toy with this question. "The artist," he writes in his first book, "is the man without content, who has no other identity than a perpetual emerging out of the nothingness of expression" (MC, 55). In his second book, the same idea (and the same pathos) returns with the claim that the artist takes "to its extreme consequences the principle of loss and self-dispossession" by "becoming an object . . . a living corpse . . . a creature essentially nonhuman and antihuman" (S, 50). His portrait of the artist as a hollow man is grounded in a new philosophy of life that departs from the life-philosophy of the late nineteenth and early twentieth centuries, which is described in his third book as an "attempt to gather 'life' into a 'pure experience' . . . [and] to capture this lived experience as introspectively revealed in its preconceptual immediacy" (IH, 40). He claims that basing one's philosophy, art, or life on one's "stream of consciousness" or "rhapsody of perceptions," as happens in Husserl's phenomenology, is a futile reaction against the gradual erosion of a meaningful "inner life" in our time, an inability to come to terms with what he calls the "destruction of experience." "Modern man," he observes, "makes his way home in the evening wearied by a jumble of events, but however entertaining or tedious, unusual or commonplace, harrowing or pleasurable they are, none of them will have become experience" (IH, 16). Instead of searching nostalgically for our diminishing psychic existence, instead of mourning our dwindling inner consciousness, Agamben champions here a spectral form of life that chooses to embrace, almost celebrate, its inward void. I often tried, with little success, to make some practical sense of this line of thought, until I read this passage from Kafka's diary:

> Many years ago I sat one day, in a sad enough mood, on the slope of the Laurenziberg [a hill at the center of Prague]. I went over the wishes that I wanted to realize in life. I found that the most important or the most delightful was the wish to attain a view of life (and—this was necessarily bound up with it—to convince others of it in writing), in which life, while still retaining its full-bodied rise and fall, would simultaneously be recognized no less clearly as a nothing, a dream, a dim hovering. A beautiful wish, perhaps, if I had wished it rightly.[28]

Kafka's readers are prone to accept his celebrated worldview, with its intricate bureaucracy and nightmarish senselessness. They are much less receptive to the elusive view of life that he portrays in many of his stories, which is lucidly defined in this diary entry as the tension between presence (life's "full-bodied rise and fall") and absence ("a nothing, a dream, a dim hovering"). All the characters in Kafka's three novels have a specific task that they need to fulfill or a particular role that completely consumes and defines their existence. Arendt refers to these characters as "jobholders" before contrasting those "omnicompetent" persons with the protagonists, the three K.s, who are the only exceptions to this rigid literary rule (K. from *The Castle* is a land surveyor in name but not in practice).[29] Kafka's antiheroes are all variations on "the man who disappeared" (the original title of *Amerika*); they remain hovering between their presence and their absence, their form and their formlessness, abandoned in this state of limbo, suspended in their whatever singularities. These pariah figures stand for the new vision of life that first came to Kafka while sitting on the slopes of the Laurenziberg hill, like a Moses without a people on the Mount Sinai of Modernity.

We can further say that Kafka is making here an allusion to a new form of life, but only as long as we realize that this "form is empty" and that "emptiness is form."[30] The notion of emptiness, crystallized in this proposition taken from the Buddhist *Heart Sutra*, is one of those powerful ideas that demonstrates why Western philosophy (and Agamben's in particular) might be better off paying closer attention to its Eastern ally. The *Tao Te Ching*, attributed to Laozi, offers an exemplary early formulation of this same idea: "Thirty spokes are united in one hub. It is in its emptiness where the usefulness of the cart lies. Clay is heated and a pot is made. It is in its emptiness where the usefulness of the pot lies. Doors and windows are chiseled out. It is in its emptiness where the usefulness of a room lies. Thus, there is presence for the benefit, and there is non-presence for the use."[31] Laozi distinguishes here absence from presence by saying that the former is useful whereas the latter is beneficial. Whatever may be the benefit or the profit that one may obtain from a porcelain cup, it cannot be of any use unless it is empty. Nevertheless, there is no absence other than through a relation to some presence (it is still a physical cup that can be empty or not). Notice that the usefulness of what is not, in opposition to the benefit of what is, can never be exhausted. The doorknob may be broken because of misuse or overuse, but the threshold through which one passes every day will never be worn out. This is true of both objects and persons. The notion of emptiness could thus inform a potentially inexhaustible life that would be present while absent—reminiscent of Agamben's "man without content" and his "whatever being"—by associating this life with a form or a way (*Tao*) and dissociating it from the subject or the individual. Zhuangzi, Laozi's successor, further clarifies the ethical lesson behind this idea with a simple parable: Imagine that you cross a calm river by boat, when suddenly an empty boat happens to bump into yours. Even if you have a hot and quick temper, Zhuangzi reasons, you will not get angry at the empty vessel. But if there were a man in the other boat, you would probably be furious and shout at him. Not to be confused with the Trojan horse tactic of the West, the Eastern emphasis on emptiness is a prime strategy for an elusive life that can evade the scrutiny of the apparatuses of power: "If man could succeed in making himself empty," Zhuangzi writes, "and in that way wander through the world, then who could do him any harm?"[32]

Inconspicuousness and even blandness are the improbable virtues that may enable one to achieve this desired state of emptiness. To better see this point, we do not necessarily need to continue to consult the texts of ancient Chinese masters. We need only invoke a few well-known passages written by two masters who lived in Paris until very recently. In *A Thousand Plateaus*, Deleuze and Guattari call "becoming-imperceptible" the way by which somebody can "be like everybody else." In opposition to the usual laments about conformism, they claim that not everybody can become everybody, since "to go unnoticed is by no means easy. To be a stranger, even to one's doorman or neighbors," to "blend in with the walls," actually requires "asceticism," "sobriety," and "elegance," which are not easily attained.[33] Deleuze, by the way, was a dedicated practitioner of this method: his remarkable (one might say eccentric) philosophical thought never deterred him from living the most unremarkable (one might say boring) everyday life—a fact that surely pains his eager biographers. "Conceal me what I am," Viola says in *Twelfth Night*, "and be my aid, for such disguise as haply shall become the form of my intent."[34]

All of this may further suggest that our tendency to bemoan society's transformation into a lonely crowd, to criticize our separation from one another, and to dream about close-knit communities with a warm and fuzzy sense of mutual recognition must be taken with a grain of salt. One may even want to take Barthes's advice quite seriously: "There is only one way left to escape the alienation of present day society: to retreat ahead of it."[35] Since the basic premise of political thought is that we need to *come together*, the positive consequences of *coming apart* are either neglected or, even worse, considered to be the terminal illness of the body politic. In some of his recent forays into cultural critique, Agamben takes aim at electronic apparatuses like cell phones or laptops because he believes that they desubjectify their users, who in turn "become incapable of looking each other in the eye," desiring only "the fleeting and almost insolent pleasure of being recognized by a machine, without the burden of the emotional implications that are inseparable from recognition by another human being"—though he also admits that it is precisely in this process of desubjectification that we should look for what he calls "the new figure of the human" (*N*, 65–66). Although it is still not at all clear how this new figure will show its (faceless) face, it is not far-fetched to conjecture that the coming insurrection will find certain digital apparatuses as useful as the traditional barricades and demonstrations in the streets (which still operate according to the old logic of the politics of presence). This is why we need to rethink our romantic image of garden-variety revolutionaries arguing in smoke-filled cafés until the wee hours of the night about what needs to be done, and learn to accommodate, with every caution, the emerging image of today's young people, with their faces illuminated by a small screen, tapping in silence and solitude on their portable devices. They are present, but they are also absent, and it is about time that we stop reprimanding them for it.

Agamben's own way of thinking and living is often criticized as passive and even as evasive. What we tend to think of as "political activism"—head-on confrontation with the state, the law, or sovereign power, visible protest against the oppression, injustice, or the inequality these last so often perpetuate—is for the most part absent from the Agambenian form of life. Given the centrality in his philosophy of notions like potentiality and inoperativity, he may even be considered a "political inactivist." A revolution, understood as the event after which those who were previously absent from the political sphere manage to make themselves present, cannot be said to be the goal to which he aspires. Instead, it can be said that his philosophy teems with what Deleuze and Guattari call "lines of flight." Flight, Agamben explains, has a political significance only if it is "a flight that would not imply evasion" but instead "a movement on the spot, in the situation itself," simply because there is no *elsewhere* that is worth fleeing to.[36] In this (only seemingly paradoxical) way, Agamben reinforces Deleuze and Guattari's own warning against the false impression that a line of flight has anything to do with running away, with "the way in which an individual escapes on his or her own account, escapes 'responsibilities,' escapes the world, takes refuge in the desert, or else in art."[37] Rather, a line of flight is an immobile movement *in situ*, which must be internal to the very life that one lives at this place and time, as long as one manages to be and not to be in the here and the now, to be absent while present, to be perceptible and imperceptible at the same time. At its best, philosophy functions as a perfect manifestation of this impalpable form of life (maybe this is the reason that venues like the classroom and the conference rarely produce philosophy worthy of its name).

This point may be clarified by addressing another serious misunderstanding that plagues the notion of "lines of flight," stemming from a sentence that Deleuze and Guattari were fond of quoting from George Jackson, the African American Black Panther: "I may be running, but I'm looking for a gun as I go."[38] It is not hard to imagine why some people who try to resist the established powers read this quote as a justification for the use of violence. But such a call for arms completely misses Deleuze and Guattari's original point, since they explain quite clearly that what they are after is a group or an individual that *functions* as a line of flight, "that creates the line rather than following it," and thus this individual or this group "is itself the living weapon it forges," which is the reason it has no need to steal an actual gun.[39] You can be (rather than search for) a line of flight. You do not need to grab a weapon, because you may become one through your form of life. The ultimate question in this chapter, then, is how can this Agambenian "movement on the spot, in the situation itself," forge itself into such a living weapon?

Life and Violence

Here we must finally confront the loaded association of life and violence. These two words are etymological neighbors in many languages. Compare, for example, *vita* and *vis* in Latin, *bios* and *bia* in Greek, *jivah* and *jiya* in Sanskrit, as well as the Indo-European **guiuos* and **guiie* (all the former stand for "life," "aliveness," or "living," whereas the latter stand for "violence," "force," or "strength"). But if we try to trace a theoretical rather than a linguistic genealogy of this decisive link, we will sooner or later need to confront a founding text, which is actually a phantom. In a letter to Gershom Scholem from April 17, 1920, Benjamin reveals that he has just finished writing "a very short but timely note" called "Life and Violence" (*Leben und Gewalt*).[40] In another letter, dated a month later, Benjamin promises to send his friend a copy of the essay, now titled "Violence and Life," but Scholem claims that he never got it.[41] Scholars believe that this lost text was planned to be part of a larger work on the subject of politics, the sole sure survivor of which is "Critique of Violence" from 1921. Perhaps, "Critique of Violence" *is* "Violence and Life." But even if there were a separate lost text, the surviving essay must stand at the center of our considerations.

The way Agamben sees it, "the aim of [Benjamin's] essay is to ensure the possibility of a violence (the German term *Gewalt* also means simply power) that lies absolutely 'outside' (*außerhalb*) and 'beyond' (*jenseits*) the law and that, as such, can shatter the dialectic between lawmaking violence and law preserving violence (*rechtsetzende und rechtserhaltende Gewalt*). Benjamin calls this other figure of violence 'pure' (*reine Gewalt*) or 'divine,' and, in the human sphere, 'revolutionary'" (*SE*, 53). An act of pure violence is a very peculiar one, since it has nothing whatsoever to do with the law: it is not meant to transgress or oppose a law (as in criminal activity or civil disobedience); it is not meant to preserve or uphold a law (as in regular police enforcement or special military rule); and it is not meant to create or make a law (as in political revolution or aggressive protest). In fact, pure violence is not meant to achieve any particular end, and thus it cannot be justified by what it is supposed to achieve. A routine violent act that is not "pure" is often perceived as legitimate as long as it has a justified outcome (as in the concept of a "just war"). By contrast, "pure violence" is the name Benjamin gives in the first paragraph of his essay to the kind of human actions that exist "within the sphere of means themselves, without regard for the ends they serve."[42] How then can we trace an act of pure violence in the world as we know it? Where can we find this special type of violence that Agamben conceives "as the extreme political object, as the 'thing' of politics" (SE, 59)?

So far, we have seen what pure violence is *not*: to summarize, it is related neither to a law nor to an end. The difficult part, which will take us to the limit of Agamben's interpretation of this elusive Benjaminian notion, is to find a way to explain pure violence in unequivocally positive terms. Agamben's first and most daring attempt to do so is to be found in "On the Limits of Violence," an early essay where he claims, quite surprisingly, that the only violence that can truly be seen as "pure" is *sacred* violence.[43] He explains there that the function of primitive sacrificial rituals is to allow the profane continuum to break down and to enable time to be "reborn." Unlike typical modern revolutionary violence, the primitive rites of sacred violence are not meant to destroy the old order for good or to establish a new and lasting world order but to repeatedly regenerate the community, to make it possible for one cycle to end and another to begin. (As we have seen, the story of such sacrifice is the basis for *The Rite of Spring*.) Agamben considers this phenomenon of revitalization to be a kind of self-violence or self-sacrifice that the community periodically inflicts upon itself in order to begin, time and again, anew. He thus writes about this "violence that experiences its own self-negation in the negation of the other, and carries the consciousness of its own death in the other's death."[44] Neither the hypocritical convenience that stands behind this justification of the physical killing of a sacrificial victim as reflecting one's own consciousness of death, nor the dubious perception of the negation of the other as a self-negation, escapes the scrutiny of Agamben himself, who dedicated pivotal passages of his future books to a full-on battle against this myth of the sacred. Pure violence never again finds its proper manifestation as sacred violence in his work.[45]

It is therefore also surprising to discover that Arendt explicitly refers to Agamben's early conception of the sacred in a footnote from *On Violence* (she apparently managed to read Agamben's essay, which the young philosopher sent her in the original Italian).[46] At the end of the first chapter of her book, after a long diatribe against Sartre's and Fanon's glorification of violence, she concedes that there may be times during which violent acts can disrupt predictable, automatic, or thoughtless behavior and interrupt the continuous chronological "progress" of history, though, she adds, such a theoretical argument is yet to be made. This is the point where she makes a nod to Agamben's essay, but only in the later, German edition of the book, which she retitled *Macht und Gewalt* (Power and Violence).[47] Arendt's central aim is to show that the opposite of violence is not nonviolence but power. She characterizes violence as instrumental in its nature, as only the means to an end that can be pursued by a single agent, whereas power is conceived as action in concert, as a sharing of words and deeds that has no particular end in mind and that does not necessarily correspond to any particular law (recall in this context Benjamin's definition of pure violence). One of the theoretical targets of Arendt's critique is a bastardized version of Nietzsche's and Bergson's philosophies of life, shared by many on both the radical Left and Right, which led to the belief that violence is "creative," that it arises from inescapable "biological" processes, and that it is therefore inextricably linked to the "sheer factuality of living."[48] (This is the other, extreme side of early life-philosophy: while some reduced life to the mere fancies of a solitary psyche, others downgraded it to the pure labor of a single soma.) It is hard to see how the young Agamben's idea of sacred violence can escape its association with this problematic line of thinking—which treats life as what he would later call "bare life"—thus making Arendt's footnote all the more puzzling.

The intricate link between life and violence remains unexplained until we take into account more esoteric clues scattered in the writings of Benjamin, Arendt, and Agamben, clues that point toward a special form of life that entails a novel understanding of pure violence. Consider, for example, the curious aside that Arendt makes toward the end of her book: "For better or worse—and I think there is every reason to be fearful as well as hopeful—the really new and potential revolutionary class in society will consist of intellectuals, and their potential power, as yet unrealized, is very great, perhaps too great for the good of mankind. But these are speculations."[49] We can also find an echo of this idea, which one may call "intellectual violence," in Agamben's early essay. Following squarely in Arendt's footsteps, he begins by admitting that, on the face of it, any link between violence and politics seems contradictory, because politics is the sphere of language, which has to do with the power of persuasion—a power from which brute violence is strictly excluded. Nevertheless, Agamben argues that today we are witnessing with our own eyes the emergence of a new phenomenon that he calls "linguistic violence."[50] Probably the most obvious example of the way our modern age transforms the apparatus of language into a special form of violence is propaganda (after the two world wars, we have come to prefer the terms "public relations" or "advertising"). Violence becomes an integral part of language the moment the latter crosses the thin line between rational persuasion and psychological manipulation. Lately it has become clear that certain acts that were traditionally labeled "violent"—from "independent" terrorist attacks to "established" wars—are nothing but twisted means of persuasion or manipulation of public opinion. Notice, also, that many conversations (that make use of language) and battles (that make use of brute force) decreasingly involve face-to-face confrontation and rely ever more on proxies and mediums that eliminate the presence in the same place of the quarreling parties. The crucial thing here is that linguistic means and violent means—which to Arendt's mind were separate—enter a zone of indetermination, where expressions like "linguistic violence" or "intellectual violence" no longer appear to be contradictory in the least. Agamben further claims that even the modern world of letters is suffused with the sort of powerful linguistic violence that led Plato to call for the banning of poetry from the Greek city. For example, he treats the Marquis de Sade as an author who exercised, by means of his writings, a potent form of linguistic violence. This intellectual violence, Sade predicted, "would go on having perpetual effect, in such a way that so long as I lived, at every hour of the day and as I lay sleeping at night, I would be constantly the cause of a particular disorder, and that this disorder might broaden to the point where it brought about a general corruption so universal or a disturbance so formal that its effects would still be felt even after my life was over."[51]

The hypothesis that I now advance is that the field of human actions that may be called "intellectual violence" or "linguistic violence" can merge with what Benjamin calls "pure violence." To see this point, let us finally turn to the "thing itself," the very text of "Critique of Violence" that I have been deliberately ignoring thus far. In it, Benjamin describes "divine" violence (the heavenly manifestation of "pure violence") as certain acts of God that have nothing to do with laws or boundaries, acts that are not meant as his simplistic retribution for the wrongdoings of the people. Such divine acts are supposed to provoke neither fear nor guilt but rather expiation or atonement. When humans witness an act of divine violence, they usually change their ways, their minds and hearts, but not because of the threat that breaking God's word will lead to dire consequences. Though divine violence can certainly be lethal, its aim is not the bloody annihilation of the bare lives of its victims but, first and foremost, the transformation of the form of life of those who remain alive.[52]

Benjamin's only example of divine violence is the biblical story of Korah and his followers, who rebelled against Moses and were consequently swallowed alive by the earth. But I think that an even more illustrative example is the story of Jonah, to whom Scholem dedicated an essay from 1919 that could very well be the model for Benjamin's conception of divine violence. Scholem explains there that what is so striking about the Book of Jonah is that it substitutes law for justice. Since it contains very little concrete prophecy, it is essentially a "pedagogical" or "didactic" book: "A human being is taught a lesson about the order of what is just. And there is indeed no figure more representative for the teacher than God himself, nor one more representative for the student than the prophet."[53] Jonah's rebellion against God and his subsequent expiation (after spending three days and three nights inside the belly of a whale) furnish a perfect case of the education of the prophet, who is presented to the reader, according to Scholem, as "a childlike person."[54]

To return to Benjamin's essay, we can now better understand his decision to follow his explication of divine violence with a very important, and much neglected, proposition: "This divine violence," he writes, "is not only attested by the religious tradition but is also found in present-day life in at least one sanctioned manifestation. Educative violence [*erzieherische Gewalt*], which in its perfect form stands outside the law, is one of its manifestations."[55] How are we to understand "educative violence"? In the narrow sense, it can stand for the (rather ineffective and controversial) violent measures—from spanking to detention and beyond—used by teachers or parents in order to achieve their pedagogical goals. But isn't it possible to define in a more general way any effective type of education as a form of pure, immediate, and bloodless violence, which appeals neither to a law nor to an end but to a different way of thinking and living? Of course, education in this sense goes far beyond what we tend to reduce to "formal education" within the confines of the "education system." The state's monopoly on educative violence in the past two centuries is quite impressive but is far from complete. Moreover, classroom education, with its fixation on the presence of a teacher and a student one in front of the other, is clearly not the only good method of influencing the ideas and actions of persons. From this perspective, education can be more or less distinguished from indoctrination into an explicit or implicit set of laws or rules, which normally has a particular end in mind. Educating can also be seen as an activity that one performs on oneself, even before it is performed by an external teacher. The care of the self, as Foucault demonstrates, may be more significant than any exterior imposition. Our positive model here is the autodidact, the self-taught person, who is perhaps the pure incarnation of what Agamben calls "self-violence." In short, any linguistic or intellectual endeavor, any human deed or act, that has the power to make or remake a human being, that allows one to see or do things differently, that has some ethical or political effect, that revolutionizes the way we think and live has in this sense an educative power. Of course, the unalloyed violence of language, education, and the intellect can be, and is, exploited to the nth degree (for example, when the thinker is transformed into the professor, or when the care of the self is transformed into disciplinary methods). Then we no longer deal with pure, potential means but with just another type of tool whose aim is the same sorry end that we call "domination." This is probably why Arendt says that, concerning intellectuals, she is fearful as much as she is hopeful.

What Arendt calls "power" is ultimately inseparable from what Benjamin calls "pure violence" and from what Agamben calls the "potentiality of thought," as long as these notions are understood in their intellectual, linguistic, or educative manifestations. If we follow this lead, it becomes apparent why the opposite of bloody wars is not peace but what we sometimes call "cultural war," which can be understood as the pure form of civil war, or as the continuation of war by means without end. Here the guiding question is not *whether* we are going to live but *how* we are going to live. The true threat is not necessarily death but a different way of life, which is, when push comes to shove, the only thing that is worth fighting for (or against). But it is also important not to forget Arendt's warning that "words used for the purpose of fighting lose their quality of speech; they become clichés," which then leads to what Benjamin calls an "impotent language, degraded to pure instrument."[56] To repeat, linguistic, intellectual, or educative violence can properly be called "pure" only if it remains within a sphere of means that is not directed at a particular or ultimate end, only if *logos* is not conflated with *nomos*. If these conditions are met, pure violence becomes the manifestation of a form of life: of a life for which what is at stake in its way of living is living itself, while what is at stake in the fact that this life is alive is its way of life.[57]

How to Imagine a Form of Life

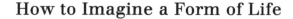

If for Wittgenstein doing philosophy meant running up against the limits of language, for Agamben it mainly has to do with running up against the limits of interpretation. As Agamben analyzes a text, he always tries to locate in it a point that is susceptible to development, until a moment comes when he encounters a limit, when he realizes that the next step can no longer be ascribed with good faith to the author under investigation. "Although," he writes, "this is a particularly happy moment for the interpreter, he knows that it is now time to abandon the text that he is analyzing and to proceed on his own" (*WA*, 13). In the same way, this chapter (and this book as a whole) is an attempt to apply Agamben's interpretive method to his own writings: to take his ideas in new and unforeseen directions, to run up against *their* limits rather than to merely reiterate, compare, or attack them as is. This approach stems from the realization that even more than the concept of life, form of life is a notion with notorious resistance to philosophical explication (it suffers from what may be called a surplus of the signified over the signifier). For a writer for whom "doctrine may legitimately be exposed only in the form of interpretation," for whom philosophy and philology always touch one another, work on the topic of form of life presents a special difficulty (*ST*, 7). It suddenly makes you aware that you "no longer have a floor under your feet," as Agamben admitted in an interview from 2004.[1] The investigation dedicated to this paramount subject is to be the final part of his *Homo Sacer* series. Although this installment is still in the making as these lines are being written, it will hopefully prove that the necessary ground was eventually discovered (apparently through an analysis of monasticism, liturgy, and subjectivity). There are certain times when certain texts should be left to speak for themselves; they do not require someone else to speak for them. If we follow Benjamin's distinction between commentary and critique, it seems right to view Agamben's growing work (and not only its future coda) as a "burning funeral pyre" and claim that the task of the critical interpreter is not to be "left with wood and ashes as the sole object of his analysis" but to inquire about "the truth whose living flame goes on burning over the heavy logs of the past, and the light ashes of life gone by."[2] In a way, the text that you are presently reading may only be an afterthought to what has been written, or maybe even a prethought to what is still to be written. I invite you, therefore, to abandon the context of Agambenian interpretations in which we have moved up until now in order to approach the subject of form of life in a new and more direct way. Doing philosophy without a solid textual ground may have a liberating effect, though it might very easily also result in free fall. This is a risk that I am willing to take, because it seems that our principal theoretical question—how to imagine a form of life—clamors for an answer in the same way that an exigent situation demands immediate action. Given the circumstances, a single, unified, and conclusive answer has been relinquished for the sake of the following theses, which may be compared to recently seeded flowerpots: some will grow plants; some will not. But they are all susceptible to development with a little attention and care on the reader's part.

ב

There are two forces in this world that propel our lives in opposite directions: the first is the power *over* life, and the second is the power *of* life. On the one hand, "biopower" is understood by Agamben as the first force, as the incessant attempt to strip life of its form and reduce it to bare life, to the mere fact of being alive, and thus to empty it of its own power. On the other hand, biopower may also be presented as a force that is internal or immanent to a life that is always understood as a form, a way, or a manner of living; therein lies its power. Whereas in the first process, life cedes its powers to external forces, in the second, those external forces become powerless in the face of life. If the first force does its best to depoliticize our lives in such a way that only the fact *that* we are alive persists as its main concern, the second politicizes our lives because *how* each and every one of us lives in any given moment becomes the central political question. We will use the term "biopolitics" to designate the constant struggle between these two forces rather than consider them independently of each other: on the one hand, the monitoring, controlling, disciplining, and administering of our lives by apparatuses of power (like the government and the police, but also the education system and economic institutions, to mention just a few obvious examples); on the other hand, our ability to fight these powers by imagining, producing, practicing, and presenting new ways to share our lives with one another. It may be assumed that the power of life is merely a reaction against the growing power over life. But it is also possible to reverse this genealogy and claim that it is actually the various apparatuses of actualized power that are reacting against the potential power embedded in the multifarious ways we live our lives. Although it is generally assumed that "life becomes resistance to power when power takes life as its object," I would like to turn Deleuze's formulation on its head: power becomes resistance to life when life takes power as its object.[3] It is important, however, to clarify here a couple of inconclusive terminological distinctions. First, I should repeat that "life" cannot have power if we conceive of it as the merely biological fact of being alive (*zoē* in Greek), but only if we think of it from the get-go as a politically qualified way of life (*bios* in Greek). Second, it should be noted that "power" stands either for the embodiment of a centralized or institutionalized entity (*potestas* in Latin) or for the efficacy of the more diffuse and less established existence shared by a multiplicity of singular living beings (*potentia* in Latin). The power over life refers to the might exercised over bare lives, whereas the power of life stands for the potentiality encapsulated in forms of life. If the former is what we typically call "the powers that be," the latter is what we may call "the powers that become," or "the coming power."

ℷ

Whether they know it or not, all established apparatuses of power tend to agree on one basic point, formulated in the clearest terms by the best theoretical minds of the Third Reich: since "no political system can survive even a generation with only naked techniques of holding power," politics is basically the practice of "giving form to the life of the people."[4] To complicate our basic dichotomy, we must admit that what the power over life is concerned with above all else is how, and not just that, we live. It is only when the powers that be realize that they have *not* managed to achieve their desired result—that life has not cared to conform to a certain form—that the opposite practice is unleashed: the stripping of life of its form (whatever it may be), this diabolical metamorphosis from caring (for the form of life) to forsaking (bare life), as power yields to violence and biopolitics transforms into "thanatopolitics" (a politics concerned with death rather than with life). The reduction of persons to bare lives is by no means a manifestation of sovereign power but rather a proof of sovereign powerlessness, that is, a failure to influence or maintain the *way* we live. Nothing is easier than to subject a bare life to power (indeed, the desire to do so is usually a mark of weakness); but it is extremely difficult, if not outright impossible, to completely subjugate a form of life to a power external to it. No matter how awesome the powers of the state, the law, the sovereign, the government, the police, or the army are, they can contain the explosive power of our forms of life with only limited success. A life completely devoid of form, like a point without extension, is a fiction. In the same way that outside the theoretical realm of Euclidean geometry there is no point with zero dimensions, there is no absolutely bare life in the actual world outside Agamben's political theory, though horrifying extreme cases, like the *Muselmann*, do exist. (By the same token, we could add that there are no pure forms of life that are totally separated from actual physical life outside Debord's theses on *The Society of the Spectacle*, though beatific limit cases, like Mickey Mouse, do indeed exist.)[5]

7

Every living being, anything that is a part of what ecologists call the biota, has a form of life that is more or less shared by members of the same species. Every organism wishes to live in its own fashion. That every life has a form is a given;

the only question is, what kind. Form is not an attribute that a life may or may not have. Philosophically speaking, we could say that form is the transcendental condition for the possibility of every life (though it is transcendent to no life). It only makes sense, however, to speak about the "human form of life" after we realize that if there is anything that distinguishes us from other living beings—and thus the only thing that approaches a definition of humanity—it is that our way of living does not need to be taken for granted, that our manner of being tends to concern us as a question, that we sometimes change how we live, and that our life is different from that of other humans. (This is the reason that Feuerbach calls man a "species being," that is, "a being to whom his *species, his mode of being* is an object of thought.")[6] There is no single element in our form of life, such as the capacity to use language, that is shared by all human beings, and there is certainly no way of life that is closer to the human essence than another, as many respected religions and philosophies still try to claim. From this perspective, the human form of life seems to be both one and many (perhaps for this reason *hayim*, the word for life in Hebrew, is both singular and plural). It is actually the diversification of the human form of life that may bring us closer to our nonexistent "essence," because the human being is a form of life being. This is not to say that "you may shape yourself into whatever form you prefer" (as Pico suggests in his humanist manifesto), because our way of life is inseparable from the facts of our life, and our thoughts about life's potentiality are inseparable from the activity that constitutes its actuality.[7] So even though the capacity to *not* act is the quintessence of human resistance, and even though one of the greatest threats to the consistency of any human form of life comes from those who think that they "can do anything," a wholly inoperative life of pure potentiality is reserved, perhaps, only to God (*N*, 43–45).

ה

A form of life is not an abstract or a theoretical entity; it is simply what we do, our actual situation, human praxis as such. It is, to appropriate Agamben's words, "the image that we ourselves have formed by our own actions" (*PC*, 158). But this entails that a form of life must face every practical constraint that one can think of. Even if it is based on some kind of original blueprint (and it almost never is), the construction of a form of life is a constant act of deconstruction. Because it operates in the real rather than the ideal world, it must confront not only other forms of life but also forces internal to it, since different people necessarily imagine and practice their shared existence differently from one another. In addition to these platitudes there is this adjacent truism: the material world also necessitates endless complications and negotiations, compromises and disappointments, which is the reason that it is no surprise that the way we actually live, in opposition to our potential life, is a muddled, incomplete, and painful affair. Many people in this world can only *imagine* a form of life, but they rarely get (or give themselves) the chance to actualize it, to make from it a reality, not just because they do not have the power to do certain things but also because they do not have the power to not do certain things. What these people need above all is not a philosophy but a strategy. On the other hand, when you look at an established institution of any kind—which is nothing more and nothing less than an actualized form of life—try to assess in what stage of its realization it operates, with what level of automatism and thoughtlessness it functions, and how much of its potentiality or vitality has been exhausted so far. We can even think of all successful institutions (theological, political, juridical, governmental, social, educational, financial, commercial, cultural, artistic, stylistic, linguistic) as *fossilized* forms of life, as the more or less empty shells of lifeless potentialities. If we wished to study lives from their inception to their petrification, to trace the bygone dynamic power of life before it calcified into the more static power over life, neither genealogy nor archeology (as Foucault and Agamben like to call their philosophical methods) would be of much help. What is needed is a different method, which might be called "paleontology." Following the etymology of the term, we understand paleo-ontology as an ontology of decayed lives that are no more, a science of no-longer-Being.[8] What all of this may ultimately mean is that fully actual forms of life, like purely potential ones, are unrealistic limit cases or extreme situations: these are only the necessary walls in between which the powers of and over life cohabit until death do them part.

1

Though it would be foolish to make light of it, one can still argue that the power over life is in its essence a banal force, that it normally affects only the surface of things, and that it can hardly achieve (and then maintain) the sort of deep-rooted, enduring, and thus radical force reserved for the power of life itself. What follows are a few perfunctory examples to elucidate this point. The first, a fact that the detractors of biotechnology prefer to ignore, is that it is difficult to imagine how either traditional methods of breeding or even the most advanced methods of genetic modification and cloning could command unrestricted control over the evolutionary process. As much harm (or good) as these powers over life may do, the powers inhering in living beings continue to slowly thrive and evolve in their complex web of diversified and altered forms. (This is one way to understand why Nietzsche sees the "will to life" as a "will to power.")[9] One can surely try to protect, patronize, or victimize the natural order, but this will always only be a footnote in the book of nature's instinctive fight for its own survival. A second paradigmatic example is the Jewish Diaspora, which has persevered despite countless acts of persecution and oppression for two millennia, culminating in a failed attempt to systematically exterminate it during the Second World War. But what this oft-rehearsed narrative tends to pass over in silence are the two instances when Judaism extended beyond its original position as a form of life (its conflation with a religious code and a national identity are only the fossilized versions of this form). What happened when this form of life, which was for the most part scattered to the four corners of the earth, settled into a state apparatus with a defined land, a fixed law, and an established sovereignty (during biblical times, and during our own times)? Anyone with even scant familiarity with the ancient books of the prophets and the current pages of our newspapers can see how Judaism has shown clear signs of decline whenever it has transformed from the radical power of life into a banal power over life. A third textbook example of the subordination of the seemingly solid power over life to the more fluid power of life itself dates back to the days of the Greeks and Romans: when the powers that be chose to annihilate a physical life (Socrates,

Jesus) with the not-so-veiled intention of subduing a certain form of life (philosophy, Christianity), the attempt was not only pretty futile on the local level but wildly counterproductive on the historical level. Because even though bare life can be infinitely destroyed, something always remains. Form of life is this remnant.

¶

"How light power would be," Foucault waxes poetic, "and easy to dismantle, no doubt, if all it did was to observe, spy, detect, prohibit, and punish; but it incites, provokes, produces. It is not simply eye and ear: it makes people act and speak."[10] This, however, is not to say that power is some obscure entity that reigns over life from above, nor is it to say that life can be inscribed into power or excluded from it. The reason is that power is neither a thing nor a container. Power is always a *relation* between some and others. Though it is not important who exactly is observing, inciting, and so on, or who is being punished, provoked, and so forth, the nodes between the lines of power are always alive. It is therefore impossible to think of life and power as two separate substances (maybe this explains why even God used to be treated as a living being, and why some machines will one day also be considered as alive). What we call the power over life is really just the power of life in disguise, and the power of life is really just the power relations *between* lives. Strictly speaking, a single individual's life considered in itself can neither be subjected to power nor be in possession of it, because power emerges only from the *interaction* between at least two living entities. And everything that is said here about the power of life is also applicable to the form of life, since the two expressions are essentially symmetrical. A mode (of life) can affect another mode (of life), but only because each mode is nothing other than the relation between lives, and these lives are inseparable from their modes of life, thus creating a circularity that is virtuous rather than vicious. In this way, the conceptual trinity of life, form, and power collapses into one being. No dialectics and no economy are possible among these concepts; they operate as a single inextricable atomic unit: the-power-of-form-of-life. But unlike those in hierarchical models, the power relations that constitute the sort of viable forms of life that interest us here usually lack a center from which this power emanates. Instead, a form of life tends to function more like a network. To adopt Deleuze and Guattari's terms, we could say that it operates according to the logic of the rhizome (like the roots of grass) and resists the arborescent logic (like the trunk of a tree) exemplified in sovereign power. This rhizomatic configuration ensures that the way we live is much more robust than any centralized power in its ability to resist external or internal attacks, because a center can be easily undermined, or cut off, or shut down. This also means that forms of life are not evenly spread out but tend to create clusters of intense, and thus powerful, interactions, along with dispersed, and thus weaker, offshoots. Yet the most crucial thing about the power relations that constitute our networklike forms of life is this: they are virtually ungovernable.

ח

To speak of a private form of life is as senseless as speaking about a private language. A way of life is always shared; the participation of other living beings is its very lifeblood. The struggle for the recognition of the way we live by other living beings, even by the uninitiated who live very differently from us, is also a sine qua non (communes, monasteries, cults, and other close-knit or hermetic groups have a tendency to overlook this second point). The survival of a common mode of living and its development from generation to generation, from land to land, is much more primordial than the perseverance of any individual's life. But this fact is easily forgotten in today's climate, where the dogma of the sacredness of (the mere facts of) life reigns supreme. The relationship of singular lives to a form is like the relationship of stars to a constellation. One can *partake* in a form (I ride my bike around town) but never *possess* it the way one does a personal identity (I am a bike rider), a right (I can ride my bike on the bike path), or a simple private property (this is my bike). These considerations may lead us to reevaluate one of our most cherished values, which is presently undergoing a process of irreversible erosion (mainly as a result of a panoply of electronic apparatuses). It becomes more and more clear these days that privacy is a thing of the past. The attempt to shield certain aspects of our existence from others is not only a lost battle; it is the wrong one. A life that cannot be separated from its form, a life where something like bare life cannot be isolated, is a life for which private existence is just an extension of public existence, and vice versa. It is a life that is always, and not only sometimes, political. Everything that pertains to our private, bare life (what we eat or drink, how or with whom we make love, how we subsist or what we consume, how we feel physically or emotionally, and other so-called domestic issues) is at stake today not merely as a precondition of our shared form of life but as part and parcel of it. In other words, what is questioned here is not really the legitimacy of the private sphere but the metaphysical distinction between the private and the public, the bourgeois division between what is only mine and what belongs to everyone. In a post-Arendtian world, we have gradually come to realize that the ancient Greeks' distinction between the private realm of the home (*oikos*), which is reserved for the basic facts of life, and the public realm of the city (*polis*), which is dedicated to the way of life, is a separation that we need to forgo, not uphold. In a post-Agambenian world, we also need to take the next logical step and stop resisting the vanishing separation between the two discourses—economy (from *oikos*) and politics (from *polis*)—that claim to deal with two realms that, in reality, can no longer be distinguished from one another. Extending the tradition of political economy, we may even say that today's world is not a *cosmopolis* but, more precisely, an *ecopolis*, where economic and political forces operate as a single field of tensions without maintaining even the pretense that they are independent of one another. This is not to say that we need to strike a balance between these two realms, and it is surely not to suggest that either the private sphere of economic behemoths or the public sphere of political leviathans should triumph while the other should be vanquished. Rather, the claim is that a realistic analysis of our human condition must consider every element of our lives as operating simultaneously within these two realms (more like the Spinozistic attributes of thought and extension, and less like the Marxist distinction between structure and superstructure).

ย

Any idea considered independently of a form of life is neither true nor false but simply nonsensical. This means that the most fundamental political question today is not who is right and who is wrong, whose argument wins in the battleground of ideas, but who is incorporating these ideas into a way of life and who is not, who is treating life as a form and who is treating it as a fact, who is using life's potential as political (and economic) power and who is squandering it. Any other division is secondary. There are only two options: either life becomes power, or power takes over life (either messianism or nihilism, to use Agamben's charged terms), though it must be added that we normally live somewhere on the continuum between these two extreme conditions and that there is no reason to believe that this tension will ever be completely resolved. We therefore need to dispel the constant confusion between these two distinct paths: we must realize that it is a standard operating procedure of the powers over our lives to make us believe that we are in control when in fact we are not, that we act according to our own nature when in fact we do not. Of course, the opposite is equally true: we often have the illusion that our lives are constrained by external powers, when in fact we are completely free. From the perspective of the powers over life, human beings are a renewable source of energy that can either be harnessed (through formation) for this or that end or that is simply left unused (unformed) like wind or sunlight. Yet from the perspective of a singular life (my life, your life), it is hard to avoid feeling that our time on this earth between birth and death is a nonrenewable source of potential energy, like coal or oil, that can be used wisely or imprudently, depending on the way life is lived. Even if you happen to believe in heaven and hell, the way you live in this world is still the sole chance you have to determine your life hereafter. Even if it is true *that* I am alive (for a decade, a century, or even an eternity), the question of *how* I will live this life remains unanswered. The reason is that, once again, the power of one's life lies in one's way of life, and nowhere else. On the other hand, it is impossible for a way of life to be powerful other than by actually living it, by continuously producing or generating it. In this way, power functions as the necessary medium that enables us to finally reject the split in the concept of life that begins with the ancient Greeks' distinction between *bios* and *zoē*, the manner of living and the fact of being alive, which is a linguistic anomaly with virtually no precursors or successors in the Western tradition. Separating *that* one lives from *how* one lives results in two completely powerless entities. Power binds *bios* and *zoē* to each other, just as the nuclear force keeps protons and neutrons together. The binding produces the power, and the power maintains the binding.

'

It seems possible to tell the story of Western politics in such a way that its true protagonist is not the fiction of bare lives but the reality of forms of life. It is not so far-fetched to assume that the way we live not only will be but also is, and even was, a prime political concern, a (or even the) decisive public matter (*respublica*). There appears to be nothing that compels us to limit the biopolitical situation—understood, again, as the concurrent powers over and of life—to the modern age. Though Foucault and, to a lesser degree, Agamben do not shy away from making sweeping claims about how everything has changed in modernity through some kind of break from the past or a rupture with the future, it is also crucial to notice that both authors trace their genealogical and archeological studies (which do not pretend to be historical ones) back to the classical and medieval traditions. In the same spirit, I have no intention of locating in chronological time a definitive historical shift from a politics that revolved around bare life to one centered on form of life. This, however, does not preclude the possibility that the question of form of life (and not just the question of bare life) indeed intensified and became more visible in the modern world. Until the historical revisionists prove otherwise, it seems safe to say that ways of living became in modernity more dynamic, plastic, and mobile—less certain, necessary, and stable. People increasingly began to treat the way they live as a key issue and problematized more aspects of their everyday existence. The result was an intricate web of novel power relations that redefined the modern terrain. The "new," that watchword of modernity, does not simply denote new ideas or new things but, above all, Dante's promise of a *new life* (in opposition to the medieval promise of an afterlife). "There are times in life," Foucault wrote before his death, "when the question of knowing if one can think differently than one thinks, and perceive differently than one sees, is absolutely necessary if one is to go on looking and reflecting at all."[11] He fails to mention, however, those defining moments—not only in an individual's personal life but also, and even more important, in a shared form of life—when it becomes apparent that without *living differently* it might no longer be sensible to even be. Since the oppressive powers over our lives are not necessarily external ("I order you to work extra hours") but usually self-imposed ("I want to work longer hours"), the potential power of a possible new form of life always looms as the greatest threat over any established power. But what some people who are dissatisfied with their predicament tend to forget is that changing life (rather than the world) is only half of the story. The new life is not just a step on the way to an even newer life; it has to be *lived through*: daily, repeatedly, relentlessly.

יא

It would be misleading to limit the advent of Western modernity to the rise of secularism as an alternative way of life to the religious one, because we then fail to account for the inner strife within the Judeo-Christian tradition itself, which engaged a growing number of factions that consider their varying forms of life to be their central point of contention. Arguably, the first cracks in the social dam that led to a torrent of powerful modes of living that is still sweeping through the modern landscape began not only with the renunciation of a medieval life guided by faith for the sake of a less traditional life guided by reason, but also with the splintering of the monopoly on religious belief into a growing variety of communities that chose to pursue their new forms of life with great conviction and unflinching tenacity. Despite the attempt to separate church and state in order to relegate religious beliefs to a private or even an intimate realm, devotional forms of life continue to this very day to maintain a decisively public and political presence.[12] Though a religious practice might be perceived as the sanctification of a form of life that is thus separated from the profane order of the world, even a hermit who lives in complete solitude cannot be said to lack a place in what Augustine calls the "city of man," that is, the political terrain on which the powers of our forms of life are being decided every day. To use a better example, to perceive Ultra-Orthodox Jews or the Amish as detached relics of a bygone, premodern world is to ignore the simple fact that these forms of life were conceived as a direct counterforce to the secular world that they unmistakably inhabit. Every form of life, not only strict religious ones, limits what we say, do, eat, read, wear, and so on. Every way of life inevitably involves ritualized, liturgical, or ceremonial repetition of certain words and deeds. If there is a single factor that produces a useful division of the modern modes of living, it is not the belief in the existence of God, which can lead to very different ways of life, but the adherence to a code of law, which may or may not have a religious origin. From this perspective it is not exactly the fundamentalization of faith but rather the dogmatization, juridicization, or Pharisization of the (religious or secular) rules that guide our fossilized, everyday life that is truly disconcerting.

יב

The rise in modernity of forms of life that are not necessarily grounded in religious convictions is still probably one of the most momentous political events in human history. We are not talking here about the failed attempt to grant equal and universal rights to all human beings under the assumption that deep down (as bare lives devoid of any form, or as a form deprived of actual life) we are basically the same. What we are talking about is the different forms of life that were previously irrelevant to political considerations and then found ways to participate *as such* in the public realm. Not to disregard Agamben's and Foucault's piercing critiques of modernity, we would be disingenuous to ignore the fact that, to a great extent, only the form of life of white, European, Christian, wealthy, heterosexual males had a place in public considerations until very recently. That this is no longer the case does not mean that certain *facts* of life (that I am black, Asian, Jewish, poor, bisexual, female) are now overlooked, or legitimized, or even insisted upon, as happens in identity politics. What it means is that new *ways* of life, which cannot be reduced to biological facts, begin to participate in, and thus enrich, what used to be a one-dimensional and anemic, and thus restrictive and oppressive, public sphere. Sometimes getting something exactly wrong is getting it almost right. For example, in identity politics we try to treat a fact of our life as our form of life, while in form of life politics we do the exact opposite: we approach our way of life as a fact (or, much better, as what the young Heidegger called "factical life" or "facticity").[13] The crucial issue here is not really *what* is one's form of life (enter the farcical parade of identities) but *that* one's singular life has (or partakes in) a form, and that this form, which has no need to be further defined, is always already a source of power. It can therefore be demonstrated that struggles that have integrated, even unknowingly, the logic of form of life have more lasting success than battles dominated by the logic of sovereignty, rights, blood, or land. Even while we are blinded by critical theory's unflagging skepticism toward modern progress, it is difficult to miss this profound, radical, and probably irreversible revolution that is still far from being an accomplished fact. That this, so to speak, permanent revolution in the place of previously marginalized forms of life (forms that always remain present in, but also absent from, the political space) does not necessarily entail toppling a sovereign, overhauling a government, or rewriting a law (though sometimes these measures are also needed), and that it is too diffused, splintered, and indefinite to be limited to a particular place, time, or people (though sometimes forces need to be concentrated in order to enhance their effectiveness), should not deter us from grasping that this revolution is real.

יג

There is a direct correlation between the growing power of life and the growing power over life. The rise of forms of life does not necessarily lead to the decline of bare lives. The stakes today are simply higher: the more power a life obtains, the more ingenious are the apparatuses designed to control it; the more value a life has, the more intricate are the tactics devised to capitalize on it. Whereas in medieval times the Inquisition and the confession were enough to keep most people in line, the modern apparatuses of power employ much more complex techniques to achieve much less effective results. If it is true that today's men and women are more servile than ever ("the most docile and cowardly social body that has ever existed in human history," Agamben claims), then why the need for all those sophisticated and ruthless apparatuses out there (*WA*, 22)? It is generally believed that in a global culture, the differences between forms of life gradually give way to a monochromatic existence. But as power grows over more lives in isolated or neglected places, the power of these previously untouched lives with their not-yet-dead forms may grow as well. This, however, does not happen because we flatten the image of these cultures in order to create a semblance of diversity and satisfy our fascination with the Other. The only chance those "others" have is to seize the means of representation and impress their own image on the planetary spectacle in which we live. Forms of life cannot be preserved through isolation—they can be challenged only by interaction, which is what a pluralistic, globalized, postcolonial public stage sometimes facilitates. Trying today to speak or listen while a million different voices call out at once is quite enervating, but this cacophony is still overcome whenever a single person attends to another and understands what he or she has to say. Every such communication or conversation, as fleeting or insubstantial as it may be, is a generator of the power and form of life. Despite the fact that we are witnessing a massive proliferation and expansion of apparatuses that are meant to get hold of our lives—from the closed-circuit television that monitors our every move to the regular television that manipulates our every desire, from the cell phone that traces our whereabouts to the credit card that keeps a tab on our conspicuous consumption, from the shrinks who dissect our souls to the doctors who regiment our bodies, from the schools that discipline us well into our thirties to the media outlets that monopolize our public domain—it is encouraging to note that these powers only appear to be mighty. In reality, they are just scrambling to recapture what constantly slips through their clumsy fingers.

ך'

The distinction between form of life and bare life is more elusive than it appears. For instance, it cannot be reduced to a class distinction, by claiming that material conditions decide whether a life merely subsists or whether it can also develop a form (this view, framed in not entirely different terms, triggered the young Marx's critique of capitalism). An impoverished life may indeed lead to a precarious life, but a precarious life does not entail the "animalization" of the human being. It is morally condescending and factually wrong to claim that oppressed communities cannot generate innovative, radical, and powerful forms of life, or that a life of wealth cannot easily deteriorate into a state of indifference, lack of direction, withdrawal from the public, and obsession about the material and factual conditions of living. It is clear that neither class, nor party, nor status—the three categories used by Max Weber to group human beings within the economic, political, and cultural spheres—can coincide with the notion of form of life, which defies the boundaries between these three realms. Yet it is better to be safe than sorry and at least to ensure that the notion of form of life will not be confused with what sociologists and advertisers (who often think alike) call "lifestyle," which is a way to define people by what kinds of things they consume, as if choosing a life were as easy and banal as choosing a box of cereal in the supermarket. The growing attempt in late capitalism to reduce the ways we live to lifestyles is similar to the reduction of love to the gifts exchanged between lovers. Cynicism (and Marxism) aside, one could say that buying a form of life is as hopeless as buying love. Forms of life do have a price, but they can be paid for only through diligence and perseverance (but also passion and joy), which must be invested in everything we do and say (but also in what we do not do and do not say), in every behavior and every gesture, in every wish and every thought, in every chore and every errand. If people were once able to pursue their mode of living in an organic and unselfconscious manner, in today's cultural hegemony it takes a lot of persistence and resistance to hold one's ground. If for the frivolous life in postmodernity nothing really matters, for the form of life in the coming community everything always matters.

טז

Paraphrasing Nietzsche, we could say that one is a philosopher at the cost of regarding that which all nonphilosophers call "form" as content, as "the thing itself." To be sure, philosophers belong in a topsy-turvy world: for henceforth content becomes something merely formal—our life included.[14] At its best, philosophy (but also art, as Nietzsche claims, as well as religion and science) allows us to find patterns of forms of life in the seemingly endless and senseless fragments that crowd our everyday existence. It also helps us realize that our manner of being is not merely the arbitrary shape or inconsequential refinement of this rough and ready thing that people call life (their so-called life). Rather, our form of life is precisely what philosophers understand as "the thing itself." (A good example of this philosophical proclivity at work is Judith Butler's notion of gender.) This is not to say that philosophers should merely act as the servants of a form of life or that their true task is to develop some pseudoscience of forms of life. Even though people treat the way they live as fish treat water, philosophers are not fishermen. Philosophy is, above all, a way of life in its own right. Until this elemental fact (which, as Pierre Hadot has shown, was an obvious one for the ancient Greeks) returns to inform current philosophical practice, it has no chance of getting out of the inconsequential mess in which it finds itself today. Luckily, when philosophy as a form of life devolves into philosophy as a profession, when friends degenerate into peers, the unique power that inheres in this strange mode of being does not become yet another one of those powers that dominate life (aside from the occasional stray student). Kierkegaard probably said it best: Instead of having any power whatsoever, today's philosophers seem to cheerfully "speculate themselves out of their own skin."[15]

טז

Like Marx, we have no intention of writing "recipes for the cook-shops of the future."[16] But a little guesswork, like a home remedy, can do no harm. The sovereign nation-state is not going to completely wither away, but one day it will occupy a place not dissimilar to that of today's church: a somewhat grotesque shadow of its imposing past. It will accept you when you come and release you when you go. Though the masses will continue to be comforted under the state's wings, a mixture of outliers, from outcasts to the privileged, will opt out. They will either join a new breed of organizations that will offer members the same or better services, or they will dissociate themselves from such institutions altogether. One day, being stateless will be treated as a viable choice, just as secular life is in our time. One day, courthouses and police stations, like today's cathedrals, will be perceived as quaint buildings to be visited mainly by tourists. Perhaps, looking backward, someone will then say that Agamben did to political theory what Spinoza did to theology. But to point life the way out of the double trap of divine law *and* the law of the land is a theoretical and practical task that has a long way to go before it can reach even the semblance of fulfillment. Is it possible to leave behind Augustine's theologico-political tale of two cities in order to establish a third one? Can we show the fly the way out of a bottle that is trapped inside another bottle? Formulated in Agamben's own terms, it seems that our aim is "to show law in its nonrelation to life and life in its nonrelation to law," that is, "to open a space between them for human action, which once claimed for itself the name of 'politics'" (*SE*, 88). In other words, the gate of law (whether it is sacred or profane) has nothing to do with the gate of life; closing the former will not close the latter (as Kafka implies, though never conclusively). The space that was once called "politics," and is now called "form of life," is like a garden with two separate gates, located at opposite ends. Despite endless attempts to expel us from this garden, we usually still manage to stand in its midst, while the gates of law and of life remain wide open. But rather than make the mistake of exiting through either one of these openings or of remaining caught up in the endless negotiations between the two, our task is to *close* both gates from within: first to give up the chimera of a bare life without form (or a lawless life) and then to let go of the illusion of a bare form without life (or a lifeless law). This can be achieved only after we come to realize, together with Agamben, that the two gates do not constitute two distinct options but lead to a single "empty space, in which human action with no relation to law stands before a norm with no relation to life" (*SE*, 86). Once the gates are securely shut, the form of life that no longer has any desire to exit its immanent garden can stop oscillating between what jurists like to call the "constituent" power of life that creates laws and the "constituted" power over life that preserves them. But even as urgently, this immanent form of life can also cease to rise to the petrifying heights of the "living law" (the sovereign) or to fall into the horrifying abyss of the zone of undecidability between life and law (the camp).

זי

Agamben perceives the camp, and Auschwitz in particular, as "the fundamental biopolitical paradigm of the West," as the full manifestation of the power over life (*HS*, 181). But if we wish to destroy this paradigm, it will not be enough to only understand it, to look the darkness in the eye, to expect that the saving word will somehow emerge from the danger itself. There are other tools in the philosophical toolbox besides a hammer. Without our understanding the diametrically opposite paradigm, without our fully comprehending the exemplary exhibition of the luminous power of life, the coming politics is just not going to come. The first step in this direction, which is already a leap beyond the bounds of this investigation, is to notice that if the camp stands at one extreme of the field of biopolitical tensions, then at the other, we find the city. The second step, which would be more difficult for some to take, is to realize that the camp is to the city what Auschwitz is to New York. If Benjamin treats Paris, the capital of the nineteenth century, as *the dream from which* we need to wake up, then we should approach New York, the capital of the twentieth century (which today is already lost), as *the reality into which* we must still awake from our current state of dogmatic slumber. In other words, what may be called "The Manhattan Project" is an inversion of the principle behind Benjamin's *Arcades Project*: it seeks to pass through what has been, in order to experience the present as the dream that refers to the waking world of the past.[17] Obviously, the fatal weakness of manifestos (including the one that you are about to finish reading) is their inherent lack of evidence, whereas the problem with New York is that "it is a mountain range of evidence without manifesto," as Rem

Koolhaas proclaims in the beginning of his "retroactive manifesto for Manhattan."[18] But while Koolhaas treats this island as a delirious dreamscape, the philosophy of New York begins with a perception of the city that is closer to what Manfredo Tafuri calls "the disenchanted mountain," where all ideologies and ideals are reified as iron, glass, and concrete, stripped of any shred of utopia and phantasmagoria.[19] And while the focus of these two architects is on the city as a built form, we prefer to see it as a lived form. To use another formulation from Benjamin's unfinished book, we could say that our starting point is a vision of Manhattan as "a landscape built of sheer life [*lauter Leben*]," one that stands in complete opposition to Auschwitz's terrain of bare life (*bloße Leben*).[20] The basic logic behind a place like New York is therefore not Nietzsche's "life *against* life" but rather the proposition at the core of Jane Jacobs's thought: "life attracts life."[21] She illustrates her idea with the help of the elementary analogy between (city) life and (city) light:

> Imagine a large field in darkness. In the field, many fires are burning. They are of many sizes, some great, others small; some far apart, others dotted close together; some are brightening, some are slowly going out. Each fire, large or small, extends its radiance into the surrounding murk, and thus it carves out a space. But the space and the shape of that space exist only to the extent that the light from the fire creates it. The murk has no shape or pattern except where it is carved into space by the light.[22]

Please note the proximity of Jacobs's account to that of Joyce: "Forms passed this way and that through the dull light. And that was life."[23] But this, of course, is a completely different story, which must be told in another book. It would be the next step in this attempt to imagine a form of life.

יח

Notes

Introduction

1. Samuel Taylor Coleridge, *Biographia Literaria*, in *The Collected Works*, vol. 7, ed. J. Engell and W. J. Bate (London: Routledge, 1983), 232; cf. Giorgio Agamben, "What Is a Paradigm?," lecture at the European Graduate School, August 2002 (transcript available at http://www.egs.edu/faculty/giorgio-agamben/articles/what-is-a-para digm/).

2. Ludwig Wittgenstein, *Tractatus Logico-Philosophicus*, trans. C. K. Ogden (Mineola, NY: Dover, 1998), 90.

3. Walter Benjamin, "Dostoevsky's *The Idiot*," in *Selected Writings*, vol. 1, ed. M. Bollock and M. W. Jennings (Cambridge, MA: Harvard University Press, 2004), 80.

4. Robert Musil, *The Man Without Qualities*, vol. 1, trans. S. Wilkins (New York: Vintage, 1996), 615 (translation amended).

5. Walter Benjamin, "The Storyteller," in *Selected Writings*, vol. 3, ed. H. Eiland and M. W. Jennings (Cambridge, MA: Harvard University Press, 2002), 162.

6. Hannah Arendt, "Martin Heidegger at Eighty," *New York Review of Books*, October 21, 1971, 50–54.

7. Ibid.

8. Ferdinand de Saussure, *Course in General Linguistics*, trans. A. Riedlinger (LaSalle, IL: Open Court), 15; cf. *S*, 152–57.

9. Ludwig Wittgenstein, *Philosophical Investigations*, trans. G. E. M. Anscombe (Oxford: Blackwell, 1997), 8; see David Kishik, *Wittgenstein's Form of Life* (London: Continuum, 2008).

10. See Adriano Sofri, "Un'idea di Giorgio Agamben," *Reporter*, November 9–10, 1985, 32–33.

11. Giorgio Agamben, "Gli intellettuali e la menzogna," *Prospettive settanta* (October–December 1975): 76–78 (my translation).

12. Musil, *Man Without Qualities*, 399.

13. Walter Benjamin, "The Work of Art in the Age of Reproducibility (Third Ver-

sion)," in *Selected Writings*, vol. 4, ed. M. W. Jennings (Cambridge, MA: Harvard University Press, 2006), 270.

14. F. Scott Fitzgerald, *This Side of Paradise* (New York: Penguin, 1996), 95–96.

15. Saint Augustine, *The City of God Against the Pagans*, trans. R. W. Dyson (Cambridge: Cambridge University Press, 1998), 554.

16. Guy Debord, *Complete Cinematic Work*, trans. K. Knabb (Oakland, CA: AK Press, 2003), 187.

Chapter 1

1. John Milton, *Paradise Lost* (London: Penguin, 2000), 4.

2. Aristotle, *Metaphysics*, in *The Basic Works of Aristotle*, ed. R. McKeon (New York: Random House, 1941), 712 (993b11).

3. Thomas Hobbes, *Leviathan* (New York: Touchstone, 1997), 132. A reproduction of the book's frontispiece is readily available online.

4. Ibid., 100.

5. Friedrich Nietzsche, *Thus Spoke Zarathustra*, in *The Portable Nietzsche*, ed. Walter Kaufmann (New York: Penguin, 1976), 162.

6. *HS*, 125; Horst Bredekamp, "Thomas Hobbes's Visual Strategies," in *The Cambridge Companion to Hobbes's Leviathan*, ed. P. Springborg (New York: Cambridge University Press, 2007), 41.

7. Thomas Hobbes, *On the Citizen* (Cambridge: Cambridge University Press, 1998), 142–43.

8. Gershom Scholem, *On the Kabbalah and Its Symbolism* (New York: Schocken Books, 1996), 200–201.

9. Hobbes, *Leviathan*, 132.

10. See Gil Anidjar, *Semites: Race, Religion, Literature* (Stanford: Stanford University Press, 2007).

11. See Michael Hardt and Antonio Negri, *Empire* (Cambridge, MA: Harvard University Press, 2001).

12. See Roberto Esposito, *Bios: Biopolitics and Philosophy*, trans. T. Campbell (Minneapolis: University of Minnesota Press, 2008).

13. Michel Foucault, *The Birth of Biopolitics*, trans. G. Burchell (Basingstoke, UK: Palgrave, 2008), 76.

14. Michel Foucault, "Dream, Imagination, and Existence," in *Dream and Existence* (Seattle: Review of Existential Psychology & Psychiatry, 1986), 31.

15. Franz Kafka, "On Parables," in *The Penguin Complete Short Stories of Franz Kafka*, ed. N. N. Glatzer (London: Allen Lane, 1983), 457.

16. Richard A. Watson, *Descartes's Ballet: His Doctrine of Will & Political Philosophy* (South Bend, IN: St. Augustine's Press, 2007). The full account of *The Birth of Peace* that follows can be found in Watson's translation of the libretto in this book.

17. Plato, *Cratylus*, in *Complete Works*, ed. J. M. Cooper (Indianapolis: Hackett, 1997), 124 (406d–407c).

18. André Levinson, "The Spirit of the Classic Dance," in *Dance as a Theatre Art*, ed. S. J. Cohen (Princeton: Princeton Book Company, 1992), 117.

19. See Lilian Karina and Marion Kant, *Hitler's Dancers: German Modern Dance and the Third Reich* (New York: Berghahn Books, 2003), 101.

20. Romola Nijinsky, *Nijinsky* (New York: Simon and Schuster, 1980), 424–25.

21. Peter F. Ostwald, *Vaslav Nijinsky: A Leap into Madness* (New York: Carol Publishing Group, 1991), 279.

22. Romola Nijinsky, *The Last Years of Nijinsky* (New York: Simon and Schuster, 1980), xiv. A reproduction of this photo appears in a new edition of Agamben's *Idea della prosa* (Macerata: Quodlibet, 2002).

23. Giorgio Agamben, "Le corps à venir," *Les saisons de la danse* 292 (May 1997): 6 (my translation).

24. Baruch Spinoza, *The Ethics; Treatise on the Emendation of the Intellect; Selected Letters*, trans. S. Shirley (Indianapolis: Hackett, 1992), 106.

25. The allusion here is to Heidegger's approach to metaphysics, as discussed in Agamben's *S*, 156.

26. Gilles Deleuze, *Spinoza, Practical Philosophy*, trans. R. Hurley (San Francisco: City Lights Books, 1988), 12–13.

27. Gilles Deleuze, *Expressionism in Philosophy: Spinoza*, trans. M. Joughin (New York: Zone Books, 1990), 11.

28. Harry A. Wolfson, *The Philosophy of Spinoza* (New York: Schocken Books, 1969), 66.

29. Spinoza, *The Ethics*, 177.

30. Ibid., 102.

31. See Steven Nadler, *Spinoza: A Life* (Cambridge: Cambridge University Press, 1999), 27, 42.

32. Carl Schmitt, *The Leviathan in the State Theory of Thomas Hobbes*, trans. G. Schwab and E. Hilfstein (Westport, CT: Greenwood Press, 1996), 57–58.

33. Quoted in Walter Benjamin, "The Author as Producer," in *Selected Writings*, vol. 2, pt. 2, ed. M. W. Jennings, H. Eiland, and G. Smith (Cambridge, MA: Harvard University Press, 2005), 773.

34. Giorgio Agamben, *La potenza del pensiero: saggi e conferenze* (Vicenza: N. Pozza, 2005).

35. *ME*, 9 (translation amended). Cf. Giorgio Agamben, *Mezzi senza fine: note sulla politica* (Turin: Bollati Boringhieri, 1996), 17.

36. Hannah Arendt, *The Life of the Mind: Thinking* (New York: Harcourt Brace, 1981), 71–72.

37. Friedrich Nietzsche makes this argument in *Daybreak: Thoughts on the Prejudices of Morality*, trans. R. J. Hollingdale (Cambridge: Cambridge University Press, 1997), 98.

38. Arendt, *Life of the Mind*, 176.

39. Ibid., 177.

40. Aristotle, *Metaphysics*, 880 (1072b27).

41. See Ulrich Raulff, "Interview with Giorgio Agamben—Life, a Work of Art Without an Author," *German Law Journal* 5 (May 2004): 613.

Chapter 2

1. Nietzsche, *Thus Spoke Zarathustra*, 221. This and subsequent translations in this section were amended only by capitalizing *Life* and *Wisdom*.

2. Ibid.

3. Ibid., 337.

4. Ibid., 338.

5. Ibid., 338–39.

6. Laurence Lampert, *Nietzsche's Teaching: An Interpretation of "Thus Spoke Zarathustra"* (New Haven, CT: Yale University Press, 1986), 238; Michael Platt, "What Does Zarathustra Whisper in Life's Ear?," *Nietzsche-Studien* 17 (1988): 185–86; David Goicoechea, "Zarathustra, Nihilism, and the Drama of Wisdom," in *Nietzsche and the Rhetoric of Nihilism: Essays on Interpretation, Language and Politics*, ed. T. Darby, B. Egyed, and B. Jones (Ottawa: Carleton University Press, 1989), 188; Alan White, *Within Nietzsche's Labyrinth* (New York: Routledge, 1990), 97; Eugene Victor Wolfenstein, *Inside/Outside Nietzsche: Psychoanalytic Explorations* (Ithaca, NY: Cornell University Press, 2000), 186; Frances Nesbitt Oppel, *Nietzsche on Gender: Beyond Man and Woman* (Charlottesville: University of Virginia Press, 2005), 177.

7. Hans-Georg Gadamer, "The Drama of Zarathustra," in *Nietzsche's New Seas: Explorations in Philosophy, Aesthetics, and Politics*, ed. M. A. Gillespie and T. B. Strong (Chicago: University of Chicago Press, 1988), 226–27; Maudemarie Clark, *Nietzsche on Truth and Philosophy* (Cambridge: Cambridge University Press, 1990), 263; Robert Gooding-Williams, *Zarathustra's Dionysian Modernism* (Stanford: Stanford University Press, 2001), 265; T. K. Tsung, *Nietzsche's Epic of the Soul: "Thus Spoke Zarathustra"* (Lanham, MD: Lexington Books, 2005), 218. Curiously, Walter Kaufmann, whose interpretation precedes all the others mentioned in this and in the previous note, combines the two main answers into a single conclusion: "What he whispered into the ear of life . . . is, no doubt, that after his death he will yet recur eternally" (Nietzsche, *Thus Spoke Zarathustra*, 263).

8. Stanley Rosen, *The Mask of Enlightenment: Nietzsche's Zarathustra* (Cambridge: Cambridge University Press, 1995), 205.

9. Gilles Deleuze, *Nietzsche and Philosophy*, trans. H. Tomlinson (New York: Columbia University Press, 1983), 35.

10. Jean-Luc Nancy, "Shattered Love," in *The Inoperative Community*, trans. L. Garbus and S. Sawhney (Minneapolis: University of Minnesota Press, 1991), 104.

11. Nietzsche, *Thus Spoke Zarathustra*, 153.

12. Agamben relays this anecdote in "What Is a Paradigm?"

13. Michael Foucault, "Of Other Spaces," *Diacritics* 16, no. 1 (Spring 1986): 24.

14. Michel Foucault, "Space, Knowledge, and Power," in *The Foucault Reader*, ed. P. Rabinow (New York: Pantheon, 1984), 243.

15. Walter Benjamin, "Paralipomena to 'On the Concept of History,'" in *Selected Writings*, 4:402.

16. Walter Benjamin, *The Arcades Project*, ed. R. Tiedemann (Cambridge, MA: Belknap Press, 1999), 464; James Joyce, *Ulysses* (New York: Modern Library, 1914), 35. In Benjamin's fragment, this idea is actually attributed to Proust.

17. Rainer Maria Rilke, *The Duino Elegies*, trans. J. B. Leishman and S. Spender (New York: Norton, 1963), 63.

18. Quoted in *MC*, 112; Franz Kafka, *The Blue Octavo Notebooks*, ed. M. Brod, trans. E. Kaiser and E. Wilkins (Cambridge, MA: Exact Change, 1991), 15.

19. Ingeborg Bachmann, *Darkness Spoken: The Collected Poems*, trans. P. Filkins (Brookline, MA: Zephyr Press, 2006), 612–13.

20. Italo Calvino, *Six Memos for the Next Millennium*, trans. P. Creagh (Cambridge, MA: Harvard University Press, 1988), 12.

21. Walter Benjamin, "The Storyteller," in *Selected Writings*, 3:157.

22. Ibid.

23. Fyodor Dostoevsky, *The Brothers Karamazov*, trans. R. Pevear and L. Volokhonsky (New York: Farrar, Straus and Giroux, 2002), 246–63.

24. Hannah Arendt, *On Revolution* (London: Penguin, 1990), 86.

25. Nietzsche, *Thus Spoke Zarathustra*, 258.

26. Walter Benjamin, "One Way Street," in *Selected Writings*, 1:481.

27. Walter Benjamin, "On the Concept of History," in *Selected Writings*, 4:309.

28. Sofri, "Un'idea di Giorgio Agamben," 32 (my translation).

29. Claude Lévi-Strauss, *The Savage Mind* (Chicago: University of Chicago Press, 1966), 19.

30. Ibid., 21.

31. Alfred Sohn-Rethel, *Das Ideal des Kaputten* (Bremen: Wassmann, 1990), 34 (my translation).

32. *N*, 99; Agamben, "Le corps à venir," 8.

33. Benjamin, "Naples," in *Selected Writings*, 1:417.

34. Giambattista Vico, *On the Most Ancient Wisdom of the Italians*, trans. L. M. Palmer (Ithaca, NY: Cornell University Press, 1988), 98.

35. Ibid., 96, 104.

36. Ibid., 46.

37. Ibid., 104.

38. René Descartes, *Discourse on Method and Meditations on First Philosophy*, trans. J. Veitch (New York: Barnes and Noble, 2004), 45.

39. Gilles Deleuze, *Difference and Repetition*, trans. P. Patton (New York: Columbia University Press, 1994), 13.

40. Jason Smith, "'I am sure that you are more pessimistic than I am . . .': An interview with Giorgio Agamben," *Rethinking Marxism* 16, no. 2 (April 2004), 123.

41. See Hans-Georg Gadamer and Jean Grondin, "Looking Back with Gadamer over His Writings and Their Effective History: A Dialogue with Jean Grondin," *Theory, Culture & Society* 23, no. 1 (January 2006): 93.

Chapter 3

1. Aristotle, *Metaphysics*, 732 (1003a33); cf. *HS*, 182.

2. Martin Heidegger, *Being and Time*, trans. J. Stambaugh (Albany: State University of New York Press, 1996), xix.

3. Aristotle, *On the Soul*, in *Basic Works of Aristotle*, 557 (413a23); cf. *HS*, 182.

4. Aristotle, *On the Soul*, 561 (415b13); Friedrich Nietzsche, *The Will to Power*, trans. W. Kaufmann and R. J. Hollingdale (New York: Vintage Books, 1968), 312; cf. *WA*, 33–34 (translations amended).

5. See Aristotle, *The Politics*, in *Basic Works of Aristotle*, 1284 (1326b25).

6. Jacques Derrida, *Speech and Phenomena, and Other Essays on Husserl's Theory of Signs*, trans. D. B. Allison (Evanston, IL: Northwestern University Press, 1973), 6, 10.

7. Jacques Derrida, *Writing and Difference*, trans. A. Bass (Chicago: University of Chicago Press, 1978), 203.

8. Martin Domke, *Trading with the Enemy in World War II* (New York: Central Books, 1943), 469–83.

9. See Geremy Forman and Alexandre Kedar, "From Arab Land to 'Israel Lands': The Legal Dispossession of the Palestinians Displaced by Israel in the Wake of 1948," *Environment and Planning: Society and Space* 22 (2004): 809–30.

10. David Grossman, *Sleeping on a Wire*, trans. C. Watzman (New York: Farrar, Straus and Giroux, 1994). The original Hebrew title is *Nochechim Nifkadim* (Present Absent).

11. Benedict Anderson, *Imagined Communities: Reflections on the Origin and Spread of Nationalism* (London: Verso, 1991), 6–7.

12. Agamben, "What Is a Paradigm?"

13. See Gilles Deleuze, *Bergsonism*, trans. H. Tomlinson and B. Habberjam (New York: Zone Books, 1991).

14. See *S*, 23.

15. See Hannah Arendt, *Lectures on Kant's Political Philosophy*, ed. R. Beiner (Chicago: University of Chicago Press, 1989), 79.

16. Hugo von Hofmannsthal, *Buch der Freunde* (Leipzig: Insel Verlag, 1922), 47; cf. *S*, xix.

17. Heraclitus, *Fragments*, trans. T. M. Robinson (Toronto: University of Toronto Press, 1991), 29.

18. See Levi ben Gershom, *The Wars of the Lord*, book 1, *Immortality of the Soul*, trans. S. Feldman (Philadelphia: Jewish Publication Society of America, 1983), 194–95; cf. Charles Touati, *La pensée philosophique et théologique de Gersonide* (Paris: Éditions de minuit, 1973), 421.

19. Baruch Spinoza, *Theological-Political Treatise*, in *Complete Works*, ed. S. Shirley and M. L. Morgan (Indianapolis: Hackett, 2002), 411.

20. Ibid., 859.

21. Giorgio Agamben, "The Work of Man," in *Giorgio Agamben: Sovereignty and Life*, ed. M. Calarco and S. DeCaroli (Stanford: Stanford University Press, 2007), 2.

22. Hans-Georg Gadamer, *Heidegger's Ways* (Albany: State University of New York Press, 1994), 54.

23. Heidegger, *Being and Time*, 46.

24. Jean-Luc Marion, *Reduction and Givenness: Investigations of Husserl, Heidegger, and Phenomenology* (Evanston, IL: Northwestern University Press, 1998), 100–102.

25. Martin Heidegger, *Phenomenological Interpretations of Aristotle: Initiation into Phenomenological Research* (Bloomington: Indiana University Press, 2001), 131–32, 62.

26. Ibid., 67.

27. Michel Foucault, *Discipline and Punish: The Birth of the Prison* (New York: Vintage Books, 1995), 200.

28. Franz Kafka, *The Great Wall of China: Stories and Reflections* (New York: Schocken Books, 1970), 155.

29. Hannah Arendt, *Essays in Understanding, 1930–1954*, ed. J. Kohn (New York: Harcourt, 1994), 75–76.

30. *The Heart Sutra*, trans. P. Red (Washington, DC: Shoemaker and Hoard, 2004), 2.

31. Laozi, *Daodejing*, trans. H. G. Moeller (Chicago: Open Court, 2007), 27 (translation amended).

32. Zhuangzi, *The Complete Works of Chuang Tzu*, ed. B. Watson (New York: Columbia University Press, 1968), 212 (translation amended).

33. Gilles Deleuze and Félix Guattari, *A Thousand Plateaus: Capitalism and Schizophrenia*, trans. B. Massumi (Minneapolis: University of Minnesota Press, 1987), 279.

34. William Shakespeare, *Twelfth Night* (New York: Penguin, 1968), 50.

35. Roland Barthes, *The Pleasure of the Text*, trans. R. Miller (New York: Hill and Wang, 1975), 40.

36. Smith, "'I am sure that you are more pessimistic than I am . . . ,'" 121.

37. Deleuze and Guattari, *A Thousand Plateaus*, 204.

38. Ibid.

39. Ibid.

40. Walter Benjamin, *The Correspondence of Walter Benjamin 1910–1940*, ed. G. Scholem and T. W. Adorno (Chicago: University of Chicago Press, 1994), 162.

41. Ibid., 164.

42. Walter Benjamin, "Critique of Violence," in *Selected Writings*, 1:236.

43. Giorgio Agamben, "Sui limiti della violenza," *Nuovi argumenti* 17 (January–March 1970): 168 (my translation).

44. Ibid., 170.

45. See, however, Agamben's recent essay, "Hunger of an Ox: Considerations on the Sabbath, the Feast, and Inoperativity," where he seems to reconsider a similar set of problematic ideas (*N*, 104–12).

46. Letter from Giorgio Agamben to Hannah Arendt, February 21, 1970; letter from Hannah Arendt to Giorgio Agamben, February 27, 1970. Both available at *The Hannah Arendt Papers at the Library of Congress*, retrieved from http://lcweb2.loc.gov/ammem /arendthtml/arendthome.html.

47. Hannah Arendt, *On Violence* (New York: Harcourt, 1970), 30–31; *Macht und Gewalt* (Munich: Piper, 1971), 35.

48. Arendt, *On Violence*, 74.

49. Ibid., 73.

50. Agamben, "Sui limiti della violenza," 161–63.

51. Quoted in ibid., 162; cf. Marquis de Sade, *Juliette*, trans. A. Wainhouse (New York: Grove, 1968), 525 (translation amended). These lines are uttered by Clairwil.

52. Benjamin, "Critique of Violence," 249–50.

53. Gershom Scholem, "On Jonah and the Concept of Justice," trans. E. J. Schwab, *Critical Inquiry* 25, no. 2 (Winter 1999): 354.

54. Ibid., 355.

55. Benjamin, "Critique of Violence," 250 (translation amended). Cf. Benjamin's *Gesammelte Schriften*, vol. 2, pt. 1, 200.

56. Arendt, *Essays in Understanding*, 308; Benjamin, *Correspondence of Walter Benjamin*, 80.

57. See *ME*, 4; cf. Agamben, *Mezzi senza fine*, 13.

Chapter 4

1. Raulff, "Interview with Giorgio Agamben," 613.

2. Walter Benjamin, "Goethe's *Elective Affinities*," in *Selected Writings*, 1:298.

3. Gilles Deleuze, *Foucault*, trans. S. Hand (Minneapolis: University of Minnesota Press, 1988), 92.

4. Carl Schmitt, *Roman Catholicism and Political Form*, trans. G. L. Ulmen (Westport, CT: Greenwood, 1996), 17; *HS*, 148.

5. "Understood on its own terms, the spectacle proclaims the predominance of appearances and asserts that all human life, which is to say all social life, is mere appearance. But any critique capable of apprehending the spectacle's essential character must expose it as a visible negation of life—and as a negation of life that has *invented a visual*

form for itself" (Guy Debord, *The Society of the Spectacle*, trans. D. Nicholson-Smith [New York: Zone Books, 1995], 14).

6. Ludwig Feuerbach, *The Fiery Brook: Selected Writings of Ludwig Feuerbach*, trans. Z. Hanfi (Garden City, NY: Anchor Books, 1972), 97.

7. Giovanni Pico della Mirandola, *On the Dignity of Man*, trans. C. G. Wallis (Indianapolis: Hackett, 1998), 4; cf. *O*, 29.

8. William Riley Curtis, "A Beginning of Paleo-ontology," unpublished paper, 2009.

9. "Only where there is life is there also will: not will to life but—thus I teach you— will to power." Nietzsche, *Thus Spoke Zarathustra*, 227.

10. Michel Foucault, "Lives of Infamous Men," in *Power*, ed. J. D. Faubion (New York: New Press, 2000), 172.

11. Michel Foucault, *The Use of Pleasure*, trans. R. Hurley (New York: Vintage, 1990), 8.

12. See José Casanova, *Public Religions in the Modern World* (Chicago: University of Chicago Press, 1994).

13. See Heidegger, *Phenomenological Interpretations of Aristotle*.

14. Cf. Nietzsche, *Will to Power*, 433.

15. Søren Kierkegaard, *Practice in Christianity*, trans. E. Hong and H. Hong (Princeton, NJ: Princeton University Press, 1991), 80.

16. Karl Marx, *Capital*, vol. 1, trans. B. Fowkes (London: Penguin, 1990), 99.

17. Cf. Benjamin, *The Arcades Project*, 838.

18. Rem Koolhaas, *Delirious New York* (New York: Monacelli, 1994), 9.

19. Manfredo Tafuri, "The Disenchanted Mountain," in *The American City from the Civil War to the New Deal* (Cambridge, MA: MIT Press, 1979), 461.

20. The formulation is Hugo von Hofmannsthal's, quoted in Benjamin, *The Arcades Project*, 417.

21. Friedrich Nietzsche, *On the Genealogy of Morality*, trans. C. Diethe (Cambridge: Cambridge University Press, 2006), 87; Jane Jacobs, *The Death and Life of Great American Cities* (New York: Modern Library, 1993), 454.

22. Jacobs, *The Death and Life*, 490–91.

23. James Joyce, *A Portrait of the Artist as a Young Man* (New York: Penguin, 1993), 119.

Index

Luria, Isaac, 71

Maimonides, 84
Mallarmé, Stéphane, 31
Marion, Jean-Luc, 85
Marx, Karl, 51, 58, 70, 108, 115–16
metaphysics, 33–34, 36, 49, 58, 68, 73–77, 79, 108
Milton, John, 18
Morante, Elsa, 8, 36
Musil, Robert, 3, 11

Nancy, Jean-Luc, 8, 48
Nietzsche, Friedrich, 11, 21, 33, 45–48, 60, 73, 94, 105, 116, 119, 123n37
Nijinsky, Vaslav, 30–32

Ovid, 2

Pasolini, Pier Paolo, 8
Peirce, Charles Sanders, 49
phantasm, 39, 81
Pico, Giovanni, 103
Plato, 2, 11, 17–19, 28, 41, 45, 95
potentiality, 6–7, 39–40, 42–43, 53, 80, 91, 95, 98, 101, 103–4, 109, 111
presence, 3, 75–82, 85–86, 88–91, 95, 97, 113

remnant, 55, 71–72, 106
Riefenstahl, Leni, 29
Rilke, Rainer Maria, 11, 36, 52–3
Rimbaud, Arthur, 11
Rousseau, Jean-Jacques, 36

sacred, 22, 25, 29–31, 33, 36, 58, 66, 68–69, 77, 79, 83, 93–94, 107

Sade, Marquis de, 96
Saussure, Ferdinand de, 7
Schmitt, Carl, 30, 37–38, 41
Scholem, Gershom, 92, 96–97
Shakespeare, William, 80, 89
Socrates, 4, 105
Sohn-Rethel, Alfred, 64–65
sovereignty, 18, 20–24, 26, 28, 31, 35, 37, 40–41, 77, 80, 86, 90, 102, 105, 107, 113, 116, 118
Spinoza, Baruch, 32–39, 84, 108, 117
standstill, 51–55, 59–60, 63–64, 69–70
structuralism, 67–70, 74
subjectivity, 2–4, 12–13, 66, 89–90, 99
survival, 35, 55, 105, 107

Tafuri, Manfredo, 119
thought, 4, 6, 28, 38–43, 52, 74, 98
threshold, 2, 4, 21, 30, 36, 41, 52, 67–68, 74, 79–80. *See also* indetermination, zone of

Vico, Giambattista, 65–66
violence, 91–98

Warburg, Aby, 12–13
Warhol, Andy, 13, 42
Weber, Max, 115
whatever, 82–86, 88–89
Wittgenstein, Ludwig, 2–3, 7, 13, 26, 61, 64, 99
Wolfson, Harry, 34

Zhuangzi, 89
Zeno (of Elea), 54
zoē, 34, 101, 110

Lightning Source UK Ltd.
Milton Keynes UK
UKHW011901081122
411866UK00002B/329